4.

LIES-BERGÈRE

NILA

DEVI

Danseuse Étoile

5.

6.

Dancing for Joy

Books by Regina J. Woody

by Regina J. Woody

DANCING

for

JOY

Illustrated with photographs

Drawings by Arline K. Thomson

E. P. DUTTON & COMPANY, INC.

NEW YORK, 1959

Contents

Illustrations

Dancing for Joy

chapter 1:   To London—to Visit the Queen

"I THINK the most sensible thing for us to do under the circumstances is to go to London and see the Queen." That was my mother's voice, and the sentence was as cryptic and curiosity-provoking as anything ever said by Alice or the Red Queen.

I looked up from *Oliver Twist*, which is a very sad book, and two tears dropped onto Ruby's smooth head, making him squirm in protest. Ruby was my King Charles spaniel. I was curled up on the leather sofa in the library, and Ruby was curled up on me. Father and Mother were drinking after-dinner coffee and talking in the serious voices used only for family matters of the greatest importance. The words "under the circumstances" popped up again and again. I wondered just what those "circumstances" were and if they would ever be explained to me. Right now my parents were discussing the fact that the headmistress of my boarding school was very much displeased with me. Only this afternoon she had said very gently but firmly to my mother that "until Regina gets over the idea that she is going to be a professional dancer, it would be better for her not to return to Dana Hall."

Not return to Dana Hall? It was unthinkable! I loved school. Of course I loved to dance, too, but to my mind, at fifteen, school and dancing were inseparable. How could such a terrible thing be happening to me? Hadn't I devoted myself to my small role in *A Midsummer Night's Dream?* Had I not practiced until I did it so well that everyone applauded? After all, stopping a performance of Shakespeare should have been cause for acclaim. But it wasn't! I had been scolded. The teachers had pursed their lips and looked severe. It just wasn't done. No insignificant elf was supposed to steal Shakespeare's show, and when the insignificant elf was little Regina Jones, a lowly sophomore, it was nothing less than *lèse majesté*, especially in the senior-class play.

After the performance I dressed in my best blue frock and put on a wide-brimmed navy Milan straw hat trimmed with buttercups. I waited about to say good-by. The Bishop shook hands and "harrumphed" at me, and said, "Dear, dear! Such a nice-looking little girl to go kicking about like that. Let's have no more of it, my dear."

"But I love to dance, and I just love to kick things over my head," I explained. "I think I could kick your hat if you held it up."

"Deary me," he said. "What an idea! I can assure you I shall not hold it up."

"Kick mine," said a fine-looking stranger, and held up his hat, which I obligingly kicked.

"Regina!" my mother cried in a thunderous voice, but the man with the hat introduced himself as Henry W. Savage, a theatrical producer whose name was such that it commanded respect; and everyone stopped looking shocked or laughing very hard behind their hands and smoothed their faces into polite attention.

"Bring the child to see me when she's old enough to get a job, or better yet, come see me anyway, and we'll talk about a career in the theater." He smiled at my mother, waved his hat at me, and gave a proper wink.

"See you in tights," he called. "You belong behind the footlights, not on the lawn of a girls' school."

"Did you ever!" Mother said. "I believe the man must have indulged a bit too freely." It was then that someone told Mother the headmistress wished to see her. I waited in the victoria, petting my two dogs, who had come to meet me. I tried to visit with Thomas, the coachman, but he sat stiff and straight. Finally he answered my question about my favorite horse.

"Starlight's restless," Thomas said. "He don't fancy being ridden by anybody but you." I laughed. Starlight had a sense of humor and a strong will. He could think of more ways to unseat a person, apparently unaware of what he was doing, than the average person could figure out.

"It'll be wonderful to be home," I told Thomas. "I'm a Junior now. I'm going to room with Sally next year. We're going to be in the Main Building. Isn't that grand?"

"Yes, Miss." I was surprised. Thomas and I had always been good friends, but now he seemed different, aloof and uninterested in me.

Mother came out of the headmistress's house. She looked grave. She let Thomas help her in, and sat down beside me, pushing a sleeping dog into my lap. "Home," she said briefly. Thomas climbed to the seat, lifted the reins, clucked, and Freddie started off on the eight miles down hill toward home.

"Whatever got into you to dance like that?" Mother asked

13

me. "I'm really surprised at you. Kicking way over your head and throwing yourself about. I declare, you leaped about like a mad mosquito."

"A mad mosquito!" I was insulted. "Why, Mother, Lydia and I planned the whole dance very carefully. She's a Junior, and we did exactly the same things. She kicked as high as I did. We practiced and practiced. Anyway, everyone liked it. We stopped the show."

"You stopped more than that," Mother said. "Miss Cooke has just told me she thinks it would be better for you not to come back to Dana Hall until you get dancing out of your system."

"I'll never get it out," I said furiously.

"Then you'll never go back," Mother said. "Miss Cooke made no bones about that."

"What about Lydia?" I demanded. "Is Lydia expelled too?"

"Not expelled, suspended," Mother corrected. "Anyway, she has already apologized, and from now on will do only waist-high kicks. She plans to major in Eurythmics and teach gymnastics. There's not much else she can do. Her father is a minister, and she is in school on a scholarship."

"Lydia apologized?" I could hardly believe my ears. "How come? No one asked me to apologize."

"Certainly not." Mother turned to smile at me, and I felt my spirits lift. "I asked Miss Cooke why you should apologize for dancing. I told her you loved to dance. I admitted the senior play wasn't exactly the right time or place for such a display of pyrotechnics, but I said I had no intention of asking you for an apology. Instead I announced I was going to take you abroad and give you a chance to be a real dancer. This summer will settle the question once and for all. We'll go to London and let you audition for the best men in the business. If they say you have talent, you can study there.

14

If they say *no*,"—here Mother looked at me searchingly—"then you must apologize to Miss Cooke and return to Dana Hall, dance only in your classes, study hard, and go to college. Maybe you could teach French," she added. "You love Mademoiselle Reuche. She says you have a nice accent, and it's a very respectable sort of job."

"I'm not going to teach French," I exploded. "I don't want a respectable job! I'm going to be a great dancer. I told Miss Bentley so today when she asked what we were going to do when we grew up. Francie said she was going to be a nurse and Julie said she was going to be an English teacher, and Joanne said she wanted to get married; but I said I was going to be a great dancer like Anna Pavlova and a great writer like Hans Christian Andersen."

Mother sort of choked, and her face got quite pink. She seemed to have a hard time swallowing. Finally she asked, "And what did Miss Bentley say to that?"

"Miss Bentley looked ever so funny," I said, smiling. "She reared back in her chair and put her hands out flat on the desk and said, 'I recommend that you be one thing at a time, Regina. One thing at a time!' I think I agree with her," I added solemnly. "I shall be a dancer first and then a writer. I can write when I'm quite old, when I'm twenty-five or six."

"Yes," Mother agreed. "That's true. You have to be young to dance, but you can still write, even when you have one foot in the grave, like poor Bunthorne in *Patience*."

I nodded. I knew Mother would understand.

Now she was telling Father that she thought I should have a chance to learn to dance. He nodded and cleared his throat. Their conversation was strangely disturbing. Father looked tired, and coughed asthmatically. Every night after dinner when I was home from school I would curl up on the couch and my dogs would curl up on me and I would read

Dickens. I was quite used to Father coughing. He always did when anything was wrong, so I wasn't too worried. He had read Grimm and Lang and Andersen, Rupert Brooke, and the little John Newberry books to me, and had always coughed a little or a lot. By the time I was ten, I had graduated suddenly to Jane Austen, Thackeray, Ouida, Eliot, and Dickens, but having Father cough was like background music to my reading. Because Mother and Father were Dickens fans, his characters were a part of our everyday life. Father identified with Mr. Pickwick, Mother, with Mrs. Micawber, I, with Oliver Twist and Little Dorrit.

Father had met Mr. Dickens in 1850 when he came to the United States. At that time Father was a little boy of nine. "I ran errands for Mr. Charles Dickens one whole week," Father would tell me, or anyone who would listen. "Mr. Dickens had a lot of errands he wanted done, and I nearly ran my legs off. He promised me that he would 'make it worth my while.' Visions of golden sovereigns, of pounds and guineas danced in my head. At the end of the week Mr. Dickens praised me for my courtesy and speed and devotion to his comfort and gave me this white china bust of himself." Here Father would point dramatically to the eighteen-inch china bust of Mr. Dickens, worth at that time about fifty cents. "I was broken-hearted," he added, "but as the years have passed, I have never failed to smile as I look at it. The more I read Dickens, the more admiration and amusement I feel for the author, who no doubt felt he was being very generous to a bumbling schoolboy. Mr. Dickens was a close man with his money, but a spendthrift with his genius. His readings were genuinely great works of art, and anyone who heard him read from his own writings, as I did, needed no greater reward."

Having heard this story so many times as a child, I regarded Mr. Dickens as a living person as well as a great writer, and I touched his books—so many, many beautifully bound green and gold books—with awe. I read them with rapt interest, and wept and laughed and wept again.

I returned from my daydream to hear Mother say, "We could see the Coronation. Really, Lewis, the trip will be quite educational, and even if Regina hasn't the makings of a great dancer, she will still have had a chance to try her wings."

I shut *Oliver Twist* on my finger, smoothing Ruby's black-and-brown head, which felt like a fur-covered billiard ball. I knew what "having her chance" meant. Grandma, my mother's mother, had run away to be an actress with the great Duse, and had been made to come home at once. She hadn't had *her* chance. My mother, my own mother who had earned her living as a painter of lovely landscapes before she married my father, had also run away and joined *The Black Crook* as a ballet girl before being hustled home by her irate family to take up a more ladylike profession. She hadn't had *her* chance either! But now, my mother was determined I should have *my* chance. I glowed with pride at her faith in me.

"We can use Grandma's legacy," Mother continued. "It won't cost you a penny, Lewis. You know Grandma always wanted me to go to London and meet the Monds."

"Just as you say, Gene. If that's the way you want it." Father was choking with the effort not to cough. He wiped his eyes and then his glasses. "I'm in no position to dictate terms, as you know."

"Oh, Lewis, don't say that." Mother dabbed at the tears on her cheeks. "Honestly, I don't make sense. One minute I want one thing, the next, another." She blew her nose briskly. "However, I've decided you are right, as usual. We must tell Regina the whole truth this very minute."

"Are you quite sure you mean that?" Father gave a little

hacking cough. "Only a short time ago you were saying we shouldn't burden her with our problems, that she was young only once."

"I know. I know!" Mother lifted her chin proudly. "But somehow this business of our going off a whole ocean away from you and pretending it's perfectly lovely when it isn't at all is more than I can bear. I must have been out of my mind to even consider not explaining. Why it wouldn't even be honest!"

"Very well," Father said. He looked older and more fragile than I had ever seen him. At his gesture I moved forward to sit beside him. He put his arm around me. I was a little frightened. I had never seen my parents so tense nor so upset before.

"Regina," he said, over a paroxysm of coughing. "The plain truth is that I've lost a lot of money. I've signed notes for friends and given credit to many customers who can't or won't pay. Because of the depression and the ruinous rates of interest, this house, the business, and all our land is mortgaged to the hilt. We will have to retrench drastically to save anything at all from the mess I have made of a very good heritage. Why," he continued hoarsely, "I can't even take care of my own family properly. They have to go off to London on someone else's money. I've been criminally negligent. I ought to be shot."

"Now, Lewis," Mother spoke imperiously, "you are not to blame yourself for anything, and if you're a criminal, so is every other good man. Just because you believed in the honesty and integrity of your friends and relatives and signed notes for them and extended credit is no proof you were a bad businessman. You are a good one, and everyone knows it. Anyway, I'd rather you lost money being generous to people than made it by being a Scrooge. You will most likely make it all back in a couple of years, so there is no point in worrying about it."

"But I've been such a stupid fool!" Father cleared his throat mightily. "Just when Regina needs a lovely home to entertain in, pretty frocks, and a college education, I squander her inheritance by being 'good old Lewis, who can never say *no!*' But I'll say *no* now. Just you see!" He gave a little cough, but his heart wasn't in it. He looked better, and stronger too.

"You'll never learn to say *no*," Mother told him, "not when a person needs your help. I wouldn't want you to. Anyway, the Monds are rolling in filthy lucre. Maybe Mrs. Mond will fall in love with Regina and make her an heiress. Maybe Regina will make pots of money as a dancer . . ."

"It's a little late for 'maybes' to fly." Father smiled at us boyishly. This was a family joke. He looked much better. He wasn't coughing any more, and his cheeks were pink above his whiskers. "Well, Regina, that's the story. Your father has wasted his substance like the Prodigal Son, so under the circumstances . . ."

"Under the circumstances," I repeated, "you wish I would please go somewhere else and not tell you that the money doesn't matter a bit, and that I would gladly kill a fatted calf or at least one fat hen for your dinner."

He nodded, biting his lip hard to avoid any show of emotion. I whistled to Ruby and Vixie and went out. Their damp noses tickled my ankles. I was trying very hard to pretend that none of this mattered, that I still meant what I said as I had when I said it, but it all did matter very much. Now I had no beautiful home, no golden horse, no private school. Nothing was left but the dream of being a dancer. I felt lonely and defenseless.

I wept a little as I walked. I went into the barn and drank

in the sour sweetness of horse dung, sweat, and fragrant hay. I hugged Starlight and wept on his neck. I kissed his prickly velvet nose. His strong, rhythmic breathing gave me courage, and I walked back to the house, swallowing the lump in my throat as best I could.

I knew this was the end of my enchanted childhood. The big house, the dogs, the horses—all would be gone when I returned. *If* I returned, I amended. After all, why shouldn't I succeed as a dancer? Others had. Why not I? And when I did, I would send home to my father a stream of golden sovereigns and all would be exactly as it always had been, except that I wouldn't be there to enjoy it with him.

The week before our departure passed like a dream. I was caught up in a whirl of parties. I kissed people, hugged dogs, wept again in Starlight's mane. I laid my cheek against the door jamb of my own lovely corner room, the room where Tinker Bell had danced on the wall for as long as I could remember, the room of bedtime fairy tales told by my grandmother. I hated to leave my father in his trouble, but I longed to go to London that I might be of help.

Everything happened so quickly that it seemed as if magic played a major part in the arrangements. A lovely cabin on the *Zeeland* was vacant, and somehow, though it would have cost far more than we could afford to pay, we were installed in it without charge. Flowers, candy, fat bon-voyage letters, baskets of fruit, smiling faces, big hats, rough coats, vest buttons, tears, and laughter—all were mingled in our good-bys.

"Oh, Lewis, I can't bear to leave you," Mother sobbed, her lovely pansy-trimmed toque askew, her eyes bright with tears. "Are you sure you'll be all right?" Father held her tightly in his arms.

"May I introduce Mr. Thomas Best?" Someone presented

a slender man to me. "His brother is manager at Selfridge's. I think you'll like each other." We shook hands and shouted at each other.

A dreadful clanging and bonging on brass gongs was the signal for more frantic clutchings and kissings.

"Good-by. Good-by. What a fool I am," Mother wept. "I'm worse than Mrs. Micawber."

Father chuckled and patted her on the back. "Have a good time and give Mr. Pickwick my regards." He gave me a hard hug. His whiskers caressed my cheeks. "Everything will be all right," he said gruffly.

"Please write," I begged. "Please, Daddy."

"I will," he said. And he did, every single day.

I stood at the rail of the ship and tossed paper streamers at him. Sometimes he caught one and tossed it back. Whistles blew. The salt smell was heavy. Water-soaked timbers, rancid oil and hot metal, brass polish, perfume, strong cigars, and the fragrance of forbidden wine made a heady mixture. The band played on. The ropes were cast off. We leaned farther over the rail and strained our eyes. I could not see my father any more. My eyes blurred with tears. The *Zeeland* swung majestically about, and we were off. As we sailed out of the harbor, I stood alone at the rail. Mother had gone in search of the purser.

"Miss Jones?" That was Mr. Best's voice. Quickly I wiped my tears away and turned to him. "I have taken the liberty of having three steamer chairs placed toward the front on the south side of the boat," he told me. "Come and see if that is satisfactory. I understand you dance. Shall we get up a little concert for the seamen? I'll talk to the Captain at dinner, if you're agreeable."

I stared in happy disbelief. Could this be happening to me? Miss Jones? Steamer chairs with a man! The Captain's table. A concert? He was behaving as if I were all grown up.

Though my hair was down my back and my skirts just below my knees, he gave me the feeling that I was an unusually attractive young lady, a person to look after and cherish. I could only smile and mumble my thanks.

It was the beginning of an enchanted voyage across the Atlantic.

chapter 2:   *Ship and Shore*

THREE DAYS of serene blue weather—and then a proper rough storm. Neither Mother nor I were seasick, so we ate quantities of delicious food at the Captain's table, and I walked the slippery, tilting decks with Mr. Best, who held onto the hemp ropes strung along the cabins while I clung tightly to his arm. By this time he was calling me Esmeralda and we were discussing music, costumes, and dances for the seamen's concert.

Mother was very lonely, but she pretended to be perfectly happy sewing on amber-colored silk garnered from some kindly fellow passenger as a donation. It was to be a Spanish costume. No more curious Spanish costume was ever conceived, but I'm quite sure it was less curious than the "Spanish" dance I did in bronze beaded slippers, a flaming red rose held firmly between my teeth. I think the musicians played the proper notes, but even to me the whole effect was less Spanish than was to be desired. Nevertheless I had a glorious time, kicking and stamping to my heart's content. An extremely patient and enthusiastic audience applauded vigorously and kindly donated $82 to the seamen's fund.

For me, my success left nothing to be desired. I dressed in costume the moment a camera appeared and perched on the rail for pictures, early cheesecake *circa* 1911, causing the good captain a nightmare of nerves. When he saw me his color rose to a good approximation of an autumn sunset. I had often said "down" to my dogs, but it was the first and only time that I remember being told "down, down," in guttural German. Its sound enchanted me, and I continued to sit nonchalantly above the heaving ocean for any amateur photographer who wished to point his bulky camera at me. "Why," the Captain would demand as I paced the deck on his rigid arm, "do you not remember that rail-sitting is *verboten?*"

"*Alles is verboten*," I said pertly. "I mean everything that is fun is *verboten.*"

"*Es macht nichts*," he scolded. "You will fall in the sea and I will lose much time searching round and round for your lifeless body. Such a silliness to be making like an acrobat on the rail of an ocean steamer. Also, such goings-on will spoil the ship's pool. If you go overboard, I warn you, I will not stop and look. *Phftt*, you are gone. Dead and buried in the deep."

"I will visit the enchanted land under the water that Hans Christian Andersen described," I said.

"Andersen? And why not Jacob Grimm? Andersen yet is only a fairy-taler. Grimm, now, is a folk-taler."

"Folk-tale-teller," I was tempted to reply, but as we were safely off the subject of *verboten* railings, I forbore. Even the word *verboten* seemed forgotten before the wonder of Grimm.

The ten days which passed in happy dreamlike sequence were brusquely ended when we arrived in Liverpool. There was a dock strike on. If we wanted our luggage, we could jolly well carry it ourselves, we were told. This we did with much help from overburdened gentlemen and panting small boys who valiantly hoisted and hauled luggage far bulkier than they themselves. Mr. Best staggered to the train under the weight of our shiny black steamer trunk, settled us in a compartment, and then, still breathing heavily, served us a delicious tea from a wicker basket. Our first food on English soil. Mother and I stared happily at each other, viewing the delicious lacelike buttered bread, the knobby "rocks," the fat brown teapot, far too hot to touch, the blue-banded white china teacups.

"Delicious," Mother pronounced the strong black tea which she had permitted to be milked and sugared. I sipped mine gingerly. I had really never tasted tea before, my entire experience with tea and coffee having been confined to the cambric variety made with boiled milk and a coloring of either liquid. The rocks were a good deal like our sugar cookies, except that they had apparently been made into rough balls and baked instead of being rolled out and cut in funny shapes.

The trip to London was uneventful. Installed in a small hotel by Mr. Best, we left our luggage unpacked and hurried to Selfridge's to meet Mr. Best's older brother, the manager. He was most agreeable, bade us welcome, opened charge accounts for us both, and invited us to lunch the following day. He ended by turning us loose in the store with a guide. We found Selfridge's surprisingly American, even to a soda fountain. It didn't interest us very much, as we were not the least bit hungry. Anyway, Mother reminded me that we were in England and that it was absurd to cross the ocean to eat an ice-cream soda. "Fish and chips, that's it," Mother said. "Now, where is Threadneedle Street? I want to see the Old Lady, and how far is it to Stratford on Avon? We want to go there, too."

Our guide looked very nervous. She didn't know "exact" where that street was, though she'd " 'eard" of it. Mother pinched me. It was our first experience with a Cockney accent, and we loved it. Now "that there Stratford would be something to do with rileways."

"Lovely," Mother said, "lovely." She'd always wanted to ride on a "rileway." The girl flushed and glared. How could she know that Mother adopted every accent she heard the instant she heard it, not in a spirit of jest but out of pure camaraderie.

Roast beef for dinner that evening at our small hotel was a disappointment. It was red, but far too tough to chew. The Yorkshire pudding was a disaster of itself, and the potatoes were overboiled marbles. The jam tart must have been made in the kitchen, but it would surely have done credit to a cement mixer. "All English cooking is not good," Mother said, as if making a discovery she had assumed was confined to the United States. "I know, Regina, we will look for rooms, but before we take them, we'll eat a meal in the dining room, and if the meal is like this . . . we won't take the rooms!"

Such a wise woman. The next morning we resolutely walked past the British Museum. "We must be comfortable before we sight-see," Mother said firmly. In the course of the next few days we suffered through some very bad meals, but on the third day at dinner at Carlton Mansions, Bedford Place, we were offered superlative food and were shown a lovely bed–sitting-room apartment, overlooking an enclosed park of landscaped back yards. It was quiet, clean, and within our means. As for dinner, the soup was hot and flavorful, the boiled mutton and caper sauce a delight, and the jam pudding so rich and delicate, it called for seconds. We moved straight in, again with Mr. Best's kind help.

On our first visit to Selfridge's, Mr. Best, the manager, invited us to return and lunch with him the following day. It had proved a most enjoyable occasion. We had exhibited our letters of introduction and been carefully briefed on how to get about London to see the sights. Because our Mr. Best was due on the Continent within the next few days, he escorted us to Madame Tussaud's Waxwork Exhibition and to the Crystal Palace. Then, just before he left for Rome, he told us that he was trying to find us a good place from which to view the Coronation procession, for see it we must.

When we relayed this bit of information to our friends at the pension, we were greeted with amused smiles. Surely, they said, we must realize that not a single window or grandstand seat remained unsold. Seats were at a premium. If we saw the procession at all, chances were that we would see it like everyone else, from a sea of sidewalk viewers who had held their places for many hours.

Mother merely raised her eyebrows. She never argued unless she was convinced that she couldn't get what she wanted. Until that moment arrived, she let nature take its course. And nature, in the person of Mr. Best, turned up not one but three beautiful windows complete with balcony, chairs, pillows, people, and tea. We saw the procession from beginning to end. It was a magnificent spectacle, and one which lingers vividly in my memory. Nevertheless, it was the constant, daily meeting of royalty in the months that followed that I remember with affection. So often when we were walking, an elegant carriage and pair would drive by with Queen Mary and the young Princess Mary inside, bowing and smiling at us as if we were old friends. Occasionally Edward, Prince

27

of Wales, then a golden-haired fifteen-year-old Prince Charming, and his father King George, a stocky Vandyke-bearded monarch with ready smile and regal bearing, were with them, riding in royal state.

The shining carriage, the sleek horses, the gentle face of the lovely Queen Mary, as kind and beautiful as it was serene, seemed to me to be absolutely in keeping with the interesting and friendly world in which we lived. London was a strong, well-built city, clean and substantial. The Thames was a placid river with thousands of frisky little boats. The trees and flowers and grass in the parks were kept like the grounds of a fine private estate. Never had we seen such finished perfection in our lives. "Oh, I love it," Mother whispered, "and just think, Regina, at our table in the pension there is a German baron, an Italian countess, a Scotchwoman, a Swede, a Jap, a Chinese, and two Norwegian students, as well as an Australian couple. I can hardly wait to write your father how cosmopolitan we are becoming." I told her that I did not relish her sense of humor in regard to the German baron and would she kindly tell him that she would not have him for a son-in-law.

"He keeps telling me at breakfast"—(I took Mother's up to her on a tray)—"that you say he may marry me as far as you're concerned. He doesn't understand you are kidding him, and he keeps asking me to set the date."

"Set it, dear," Mother said blithely. "He rides very well and he takes very good care of you in the park. I never worry when you are with him."

"Well, you should," I said crossly. "He tries to make love to me."

"Oh, pooh!" Mother giggled. "Really, Regina, how can a man make love on horseback?"

"You'd be surprised," I said darkly, but she only laughed harder. Going back a little in the conversation, I demanded,

"What do you mean, 'set the date'? How can I, when I've no intention of marrying him?"

"Keep him quiet," Mother said. "He'll begin to make you over if he thinks you're going to marry him. He's a very bossy man."

"But I don't want to be made over," I exploded. "I'm all right the way I am, but I do think I'd better put my skirts down and stop wearing bows."

"Hmmm!" Mother said, and looked at me sharply. But I wasn't thinking of the blond German baron who clicked his heels and kissed my hand. I was thinking of two very handsome Indian princes who were students at Oxford. It was they who took us riding in a hansom cab and on to a box at the theater.

With my skirts down to within fifteen inches of the ground, my hair in curls, minus the perky hair bows, I felt completely grown up. That night I tackled Mother. "We've seen the Coronation. I've ridden in Rotten Row. We've found the Old Lady of Threadneedle Street"—as Dickens called the Bank of England—"We've been to the Crystal Palace and the British Museum and the Tate Gallery. Now when do I get a chance to dance?"

"Later," Mother said. "First we must go to Stratford on Avon and see the Shakespeare country. I want to go on a coaching trip, and we must present our letters of introduction to Mrs. Mond. But before that, we must have a little holiday, say at Bournemouth. Anyway, no producers are in town in July. We'll be back in London by August twentieth."

"Oh, Mother!" I was exasperated. "Not back in London till August twentieth?" Our tickets home on the *Zeeland* were dated September 3. Less than two weeks to find out if I could become a great dancer! I was prepared to weep and sulk, but Mr. Best arrived back from the Continent that evening and arranged a ten-day coaching trip for us. Such a thrilling experience, full of hard riding, tootling horns, new and friendly people, delightful inns, unexpectedly delicious food, and the most beautiful countryside I had ever hoped to see.

Hardly was the trip over than we were invited by Mrs. Boots and her daughter, Rita, to spend a few days at their seashore home. Of course we had met Mrs. Boots thanks to Mr. Best. Arrived at Bournemouth I wore a new black princess bathing suit trimmed with white hand-embroidered butterflies. We bathed from a tiny wooden ark on wheels, and I might equally well have worn a burlap bag for all the chic of my bathing costume was appreciated. I rode horseback, danced once or twice at small charity concerts, and was rewarded with conscientious applause which was far from enthusiastic. I had a couple of private cries all my own, for the applause for the six child tappers was tremendous, while a pink and white girl with a head of corkscrew curls who plodded docilely about on the tips of very old, soiled pink blocked slippers stopped the concert short. She had a funny set smile. Her teeth stuck out, and she blinked her eyes in time to the music as she danced. Her elbows were very sharp and matched her long bony knees, which were bent most of the time as if to relieve the strain on her toes.

"Gets you down, don't it?" she asked me one night. "Fair gives me the creeps, these nasty things do." She made a face at her toe shoes. "It's me last concert, so 'elp me." She went on. "I'm too big for tappers now, and this toe stuff is no go for me. Can't abide the teetering round on the ends of me feet. I'm a-going into vet training. That's something loike now. Bulls is what I'd loike, but I s'pose it'll be cows. Wot you going to do?"

"Dance, I guess," I answered, doing my best to sound professional. Until this very moment I hadn't realized that the other children on the program were being paid a few bob.

Since it was for charity, Mother had promptly donated my services when I was asked to dance.

"Poor you!" the girl said briefly. "I don't envy you none. Woiking die and night for yer keep. My mom sez as how it's a racket, but I don't care. I'm one for the cows."

"I like horses and dogs," I volunteered.

"Common, that is," she assured me. "Everyone loikes them animals. I'm choosy about them as I loikes."

"Yes, I see," I agreed, and feeling distinctly confused and extremely commonplace because I liked dogs and horses, I clasped my bag shut and said good-by.

Before I was aware that we weren't returning to London, I found myself on a small boat. "We're going up the Thames to Oxford," Mother told me. "Such a wonderful experience. Billy (Mr. Best was now Billy) told me we just mustn't miss it."

"But, Mother, when am I going to audition for someone?"

"Later on." Mother smiled happily. "No use going now in August. Billy says London is absolutely empty in August."

"It can't be empty," I said, taking her statement literally. "There must be people there. The buses and the underground, the museums. Why, I'm sure they're not all closed."

"Of course not," Mother admitted. "There are people, but not the right people."

"Who are the right people?" I demanded.

"I've no idea," Mother admitted. "But really, dear, there's plenty of time. Just enjoy this trip."

"I can't," I said, giving a little whimper. "I've got a toothache."

"Oh, dear," Mother said, going quite white. "Not again. *Not* the front one!"

I whimpered louder. "Yes, the front one."

All day long I nursed my aching tooth. Every night when

our little boat docked, we consulted a new dentist. Indeed, my aching tooth actually proved a blessing in disguise, for it showed the true quality of Old World courtesy. In each town we stopped, we were known at once because we visited the dentist and the chemist shop. Innkeepers invariably made special efforts to be friendly, and gladly prepared special soft foods for me. Perfect strangers inquired after my health and often invited us to join them on a trip to Windsor Castle or for evensong at church.

On our way up the Thames we went through many locks, and the scenery grew prettier and prettier. There was no sun, but there was a dull yellow glow in the gray sky. Mother and I sat on the little leather seat in the stern of the boat, disdaining the awning-covered deck. It was at Henley that I first had tea on the river and knew the joy of being punted along for lazy hours by an attractive boy I'd met at the dentist's office and who had promptly introduced himself as the dentist's nephew and entirely at my service.

He was nice, and the tea he provided me, super. There was a pound cake and one with raisins. We ate every crumb, but I did have a terrible time with the teapot. In America we'd never be sensible enough to boil hot water and make tea on a boat. We'd fix up a brew of sorts and put it in a thermos bottle if we didn't just settle for a tepid lemonade. The first time I made tea on a Sterno stove I burned my fingers and my tongue, but the second time I made it quite creditably and waited for it to steep in its little flannel coat. I was more cautious too, and didn't drink it till it had cooled off a bit. I was very proud of my prowess, and felt like a real Britisher when Bob said it was jolly good tea.

At Oxford we stayed a week. We visited every college, and saw Holman's famous painting "Light of the World." It was all very educational, but I best recall the houseboats, decked the whole way round with madly blooming red geraniums, rocking gently on the sparkling blue water. There I saw my first swans, shiny white and as graceful as trained ballerinas. Mother continued to patronize museums and exclaim over their treasures, but I preferred my scenery at first hand, preferably with a live boy in the foreground to give it a bit of glamor.

I was quite free of the pain in my tooth by now, and prepared not only to sight-see from our comfortable lodging but to enjoy myself. Life was looking up. When we went to Christ Church I was full of religious fervor, for the service was conducted by an especially good-looking canon.

"Whatever has got into you?" Mother asked when we had gone to evensong at Christ Church for the fourth consecutive day. "We ought to be visiting some other churches, not always this one."

"I like this one," I said obstinately.

When the service was over, I persisted in loitering about. This paid off when the canon came over, shook hands, made us welcome, and asked us to tea in his rooms the next day.

"So!" Mother said, smiling. "You certainly are growing up."

We had a beautiful time. We attended church services regularly. Every day we had tea or dinner with the canon. He showed us Oxford, gave us lovely china from Merton and Magdalen, two silver teaspoons and interesting prints and etchings. Never once did I mention dancing. I expect I was much too busy acting the part of a devotedly religious girl with a mission in life. What that mission was, most fortunately, I was not asked, but having a vivid imagination, I'm sure I could have conjured one up on the spot if necessary. At the time Mother asked me with a twinkle in her eye if I hadn't forgotten that I had come abroad to learn to dance, not to be a dramatic moonstruck madonna posing in the light of stained-glass windows. She wasn't really angry at all with my suddenly acquired religious zeal, for she was having as good a time as I was. Our canon was most generous, and we met new friends of his every day.

I really hated to leave Oxford. Never had I had a more delightful time. Back on our little boat we sailed to Leamington and visited Norwich Castle. Mother was very outspoken about castles. She loved them and didn't care who knew it. "I don't blame any girl for wanting a castle," she said, "All the comfort of a modern house, electric light, heat, and such pictures—Rubens and Rembrandts, Corots and Gainsboroughs. And the trees! Such foliage!"

If I hadn't been prepared to love England, this trip would surely have made me do so, for history was becoming real and time seemed accordion-pleated. One minute we would be in the present, snapping a light switch, and a moment later we were back in the very room Amy Robsart had slept in. Somehow the fact that the window was surrounded by fresh green tendrils of ivy made more impression on me than the bed. Perhaps it was because I was quite sure Amy Robsart must have stood and looked out the window just as I was doing, and suddenly she was a real living, breathing person who could smell roses and press back the ivy to look at the view or stand bathed in gleaming moonlight to dream.

From there we went to Stratford on Avon and reveled in Shakespeare country. Ann Hathaway's cottage was smaller and quainter than I had expected. Perhaps after all the castles I'd seen, my idea of what was fitting for Shakespeare had become considerably larger than life.

By now the letters of introduction Mother had mailed on our arrival in England were bringing answers forwarded to us by Brown-Shipley. One arrived, inviting us to a wedding in the very town we were in. In a little rural church two bell-ringers pulled the bells. A tiny page in white satin bore the ring on a satin pillow, six bridesmaids and the bride crossed

34

the churchyard on a brilliant crimson carpet. Villagers curt-sied and waved along the roadside on the way home to the reception. Ladies and gentlemen in gay frocks and morning suits gathered. The women wore wide-brimmed hats with roses and veiling; the men, silk top hats and immaculate gloves. The garden-party buffet in a shady garden with our first sight of espaliered fruit trees was a fitting climax to our trip up the Thames to Stratford.

chapter 3:   London

BACK IN London Mother took to her bed. She admitted she
didn't feel very well. Her head ached, her cheeks were flushed.
She was drowsy and languid. She dozed all day and crept
down to supper. I myself felt peculiar. I was very hot and
light-headed. My face broke out in horrid pimples. We kept
to our rooms and asked that meals be sent up. We read our
mail languidly.

Father's letters were pleasantly newsy. He was well. The
house was closed. Aunt Barb was off visiting. He was eating
very good meals at the German restaurant around the corner.
He wasn't coughing at all. Starlight hadn't been sold. Instead
he was on loan to my riding master. Only his best pupils
would ride him. I could have him back any time. Even more
touching was the news that a number of Father's Chinese
customers had come in and paid their bills in full once his

financial difficulties had become known. Others were paying a dollar a week, and one restaurant had given him a free meal ticket for life. "So you see, I'll not go hungry," he wrote. "I've cast my bread upon the waters and it is coming back— eggs fooyoung. Have a good time. I miss you, but I enjoy your cards and letters. I also have enough lichee nuts, paper lanterns, and fans to put on a real party in a year or two when we're in the house again."

There was also a letter from Mrs. Ludwig Mond, asking us to tea now that she was back in London.

"We must go," Mother said, and wrote a note accepting with pleasure. "She's a very old lady," Mother explained, "and it is only courteous for us to go at her convenience."

The day came. We dressed slowly in our best. We felt fearfully dispirited. Mother inspected my face. "Horrid, nasty pimples," she agreed, dabbing on a bit of powder. "You must have eaten something that disagreed with you. I expect it was all those delicious strawberries and cream."

I admitted that possibility. I had eaten strawberries at breakfast, lunch, and dinner, and sometimes a fourth saucer at tea. It had been very piggy behavior, but I had never tasted such luscious berries in my life.

We crept into the shiny black Rolls Royce town car and rode in luxurious silence to the Mond house. Mother and I had waved at the pension window behind whose motionless curtains so many friends were peering out at our excursion into the fabulous land of wealth. But neither Mother nor I had the energy to smile or exclaim over the wonders of an automobile, which seemed to be all velvet black and shiny gold. The roses in the crystal vases were fresh, the backs of the chauffeur and footman, as even as if they'd been cut and stuffed to match each other. Their ears weren't quite right though. The footman's were redder and stuck out quite prominently. They may have been forerunners of Pooh Bear's.

In her beautiful town house living room, filled with French furniture, pale rose and beige rugs, flowered brocade, ivory woodwork, and pastel paintings in shining gilt frames, Mrs. Ludwig Mond awaited us. She was a delicate old lady dressed all in black. Her hair was not nearly as white as Grandma's had been, though she was eight years older. She was Grandma's cousin, and had married another cousin, Ludwig Mond, in Kassel, Germany. Later they had moved to England, while Grandma's family had moved to New York shortly after she had run away to be a great actress. Eventually Grandma married young Carl Lichtenstein of Hungary, whose lands had been confiscated when he had come to New York as personal aide-de-camp of the great Louis Kossuth. Grandma had a wealth of stories to tell, and though she had not seen Freda Mond since they were girls of sixteen, a correspondence of sorts at Christmas and birthdays had always been kept up.

Aware of her fragile hold on life, Grandma had begged Mother to take me to London after she had passed away and give news of her death to Freda and tell her about her four sons, Charles, Richard, Perry, and Ferd. "Our last tie," Grandma said weakly. "Freda is very artistic, she would be pleased to know how well you paint and that the little one is to be a dancer."

Mrs. Mond was gentle and gracious. She listened to news of Grandma's death, looked at the photographs we had brought, and encouraged us in our plans for a dance audition. Her secretary hovered nearby to see we didn't overtire her. Mrs. Mond was about to send for her own pictures of the family when Mother swayed in her chair and leaned back, half fainting. Cold cloths and smelling salts were ordered, the delicious tea tray laden with shining silver and delicate china was quite forgotten. A white-clad nurse appeared quite suddenly from nowhere at all. A personal maid in black with

38

a plain white apron, then footmen in livery. It had all the qualities of Alice's Wonderland. My good-bys were flurried, but Mrs. Mond, though she never moved from her big winged chair, never disturbed the gay knitted afghan about her knees, had everything under control.

"My dear," she told me as Mother was assisted to the car, "my own physician, Mr. MacGregor, will be waiting at the Carlton Mansions for you. We will wait for his opinion, but if your dear mother is confined to her bed for any length of time, it will give me much pleasure if you will spend the days here with my five grandchildren, who have their own governess. You can join them in their studies and their games."

"Thank you," I said politely, but I felt so hot and tired and itchy that all I wanted was to go home to bed, too, and never get up again.

We arrived ignominiously at the pension, the nurse still in charge of Mother. Mr. MacGregor was pacing the hall and continued to pace outside our door as the nurse and I put Mother to bed. Mother, usually so voluble, said not a word. She just breathed very hard and kept her eyes shut. If the nurse insisted she move a hand or foot, she did, very slowly and as if with difficulty. Mr. MacGregor, whom I called Doctor, examined her, but questioned me.

"All the way up the Thames by boat?" He pressed his lips together. "Were you out in the sun much?"

"There was no sun," I explained. "We sat in the stern. We didn't even need hats."

"Delayed sunstroke," he diagnosed. "Well. Cold sheets. A good nursing sister and perhaps in a week or ten days we'll have your mother on her feet."

I babbled about my audition, about the boat going home.

"We'll take care of all that in due time," he explained. "Now let's take your temperature and have a look at those spots. They're very suspicious-looking."

To my embarrassment he peeled off my clothes himself. Then he looked at the nurse. Their understanding smiles were most annoying. What was more, the miserable eczema on my face had now descended to my chest and stomach.

"Chicken pox," Mr. MacGregor said, "and the child's most over it. The scales are drying up. I'll report it, but she'll be out of quarantine in five or six days."

Meals came up, but neither Mother nor I were hungry. We settled for cool drinks, custards, and puddings. I slept and slept, and then, three days later, the rash was gone and I felt quite well. The card on our door came off and I was allowed to go downstairs to tea. It was a special tea, and I ate my first buttery hot tea cake. I was starved, and it was delicious. I even passed up all but three slices of thin buttered bread for the delectable cake. It was the first time in my life that I ever drank five cups of tea and enjoyed the last cup as much as the first.

Everyone was so kind. The German baron made inquiries. The two Indian princes suggested a bus ride. The Italian countess offered to sit with Mother to spell the nurses if I wanted to go out for a walk. Everyone was very kind, but it was Miss MacLeod's suggestion I received with ecstasy.

"If you're quite well and up to it, why don't you let me take you to Covent Garden tonight?" she asked. "Karsavina and Nijinsky are there, dancing *La Spectre de la Rose*."

"Oh, I'd love it!" I flew upstairs to ask the nurse if it could be arranged. The Italian countess followed. "Indeed, yes," she could relieve the nurse at nine o'clock and stay with Mother till I returned home. We would then put on more cool sheets and the nurse would be back promptly at seven. Now that I was well, the second nurse had been dismissed.

Covent Garden may have had elevators, but we walked up interminable flights of stairs until we arrived in the very top gallery. I think we paid only sixpence, but I may be quite wrong. For two solid weeks we went to the ballet every single night. Miss MacLeod always bought the tickets and shepherded me up the stairs. I may have done something in the daytime, but I doubt I did anything but dream and eat.

The first night was sheer rapture. Covent Garden itself burst on me in a glory of gold and glittering lights. Boxes and balconies were filled with people in glorious evening frocks. Bare shoulders were drowned under ropes of real pearls. Tiaras of real diamonds twinkled on sleek well-coiffed heads. I saw ruby-red velvet, real ermine and fluffy white fox, marabou, egrets and decorations. Such an audience I had never dreamed existed in this prosaic world. And then the orchestra took its place. Music filled the great auditorium, the curtains parted.

I can never forget the Russian Ballet as I saw it then. Seeing it with a loving heart and an untrained eye, I saw less a dance spectacle than a glimpse of my own personal heaven. I knew nothing of pirouettes, *entrechats*, *arabesques*, or *fouettés*. I had never had toe shoes on my feet. I had no idea that the fairylike skirts of the ballerinas were called tutus or that they wore silk tights and boned bodices. To me they were the disembodied Wilis of *Giselle* who somehow had been captured from a fairy tale and were before me. Karsavina's every movement—from the first gentle rustle of her dress and toe as she woke from sleep to the picking up of the single red rose, now wilted, before she hurried to the window, searching for the beloved spirit of the rose—was shot through with unbelievable excitement as she danced. Poetry of motion? Poetry of the spirit to a young dancer. It seemed not so much that she and Nijinsky danced together as that they flowed and soared about the stage. Indeed, that magical leap of his out the window was an inspired ending, for I never even considered the possibility that the leap ended in a landing. I felt sure that Nijinsky kept on going up, up, up, as if he were headed for the stars or the moon. His leaps were so buoyant that he seemed airborne. He never did seem to land. He seemed rather to spurn the stage whenever it came up to meet him and intruded on his consciousness. That his art and that of Tamara Karsavina and the many other famous dancers of the company was one of precise knowledge, long years of practice, and constant daily repetitive technical steps was something I had yet to learn. Though I knew nothing of the inborn genius, the conscious effort or the will-to-do that such dancing required, I could enjoy watching it with my heart, my spirit, and my soul. Never had I seen such beauty nor enjoyed such music as was coupled with the beautiful motion. I didn't want to talk, all I wanted to do was to watch, absorb, enjoy, and be uplifted.

Miss MacLeod loved the ballet, and I think she loved me because I loved the ballet, too. Why else would she have taken a strange American child with her night after night? We talked very little, never at all about the personalities or personal lives of the dancers, but she did know music and the stories of the ballets very well. She always carried a score, but seldom followed it note for note. Instead, it would remain closed until something wrong or perhaps something unusually right would cause her to ruffle the pages and peer shortsightedly at the music, her finger often moving over the same bars for a full moment, though the orchestra itself had rushed on. Occasionally she would pencil in notes or a question mark. Then the score would be closed, and she would seem to be listening to something in her head rather than with her ears.

It was a strangely impersonal introduction to ballet. We were both in love with it, yet neither of us knew anything of the physical aspects of the great art in which we reveled.

I saw many ballets. Some I loved more than others, but always that first *Spectre de la Rose* will remain as something quite literally out of this world, ever soaring in a fourth or fifth dimension of the spirit.

At home Mother was getting better, but she was still in bed most of the day. An hour in a chair by the window tired her to the point of irritated exhaustion.

"How utterly absurd, idiotic, impossible," she fumed, "for me to have sunstroke in England, where there is no sun! How could I know that those dull yellow clouds were dangerous? I'm used to good blue sky and broiling hot golden sunshine."

Once Mother asked if I had been going to the Monds', and I said No. "Then go," Mother said. I didn't argue. I didn't care. The light had gone out of my life when I told Miss MacLeod good-by.

"My holiday is over," she told me, kissing me in farewell. "I have enjoyed you so much, my dear. Keep me in touch with your comings and goings. I hope you succeed beyond your wildest dreams. I shall hope to see you on Covent Garden's stage."

"Thank you," I choked. "Thank you for everything. The ballets were just beautiful."

"Weren't they, now!" she said as the taxi door slammed on her and her assorted luggage and music roll, leaving me standing forlorn and alone on the sidewalk. No more Covent Garden ballets, no more anything, just lessons and games with the young Monds.

Henry and Vi Mond I knew slightly. We had met one day when they delivered flowers for Mother from the big car. There were two girls belonging to Sir Robert, and I was quite sure there was another brother or sister in Sir Alfred's family. Mrs. Mond had called them all by name, but I'd forgotten.

"Take a taxi," Mother instructed me. "Then I won't worry about your being alone all day."

I took the taxi. I was received with less than whole-hearted enthusiasm by both the governess and the children. I didn't fit in anywhere. My French compared to theirs put the governess' teeth on edge, though she tried hard not to show it and merely folded her lips in. In mathematics I was a complete dunce. My Latin was precarious where theirs was sure. They spoke German while I merely gargled it and understood just enough to get the sarcasm in their barbed comments to each other. I shone in themes, but as I always wrote about ballet, the governess inquired acidly if perhaps it wouldn't be better and more interesting reading if I learned a little more about my subject and wrote critically, instead of depending entirely on superlatives for effect.

Games really proved my undoing. I couldn't throw a ball properly, play tennis acceptably, or master any kind of sport. I couldn't understand cricket, nor could I explain our own game of baseball. I was undoubtedly a drip, a dope, and a bore. I did ride well, but where the Monds were properly turned out, I looked a sight astride my horse in a divided white linen skirt, open-neck cotton blouse, my curls tied back with a big black bow.

"What a getup." Vi sighed. "You look like something out of a circus sideshow." I couldn't tell her because of the lump in my throat that we thought my costume most conservative. Up to this time I had ridden in serge bloomers, sailor blouse, and red tie, my hair flying wild. But then, riding in Rotten Row was as different as could be from flying over the hills back home, where I was the only rider, or in the ring where I practiced *haute école* with the horses my Hungarian riding master was training for exhibition purposes.

My hosts were neither courteous nor discourteous, but I was a nuisance to them, so they began to act as if I were not there. They didn't tease me or play tricks on me, but neither was I included in their fun. I was just something extra, something to be borne with and accepted with a sigh, like a rainy day or a runny nose.

It was Henry and Vi who woke me up to the way time was passing.

"When do you sail—that is, if your mother is well enough to go home?"

"Sail?" I asked dumbly, realizing suddenly that today was the twenty-ninth of August and that we were to sail for home in less than a week.

"September third," I said. "Mother'll be all right, I guess." I could see them cringe at the "I guess." Not their faces—they were politely devoid of any expression. But their shoulders curled in disgust.

"Too bad about your dancing," Henry said gruffly. "I think you're pretty good."

"You do?" I couldn't help the surprise in my voice. I had had no idea he had ever seen me dance, though I had danced for my own exercise when it was quite evident I was only a fifth wheel in their sports.

"We all do." They clustered around me, smiling.

"I often miss a stroke watching you jump about," Henry said generously.

"I think you'd be good in a pantomime," Vi said. "You're little and quite bouncy!"

"Why don't you just up and get yourself an audition?" Henry asked. "You came over here for one. Nobody could blame you if you did."

"An audition?" I asked nervously. "How could I? I wouldn't know where to go."

"Just look up shows in the *Times*, Henry said grandly from his vast knowledge of the world. "See who's rehearsing. Here, I'll do it for you." He dashed off and returned with the *Times*.

"Look at this! The Gaiety's rehearsing something kittenish by a chap named Stuart, who wrote *Floradora*. Got dancing in it, I'll bet a bob. Harry Boucher, George Edwardes,

Leslie Stuart. They're all casting. You go to the Gaiety and get one of them to tell you if you're any good."

"I will," I said firmly. "I'll go tomorrow."

"Good luck," they chorused. "Be sure and come back and tell us. If it's good news, we'll have a bang-up tea and you can dress up and dance for us. Cheerio."

Riding back to Carlton Mansions in the hansom cab I preferred to a taxi, I was alternately thrilled and scared. The horse's rump loomed high in front of me, the cab cushions smelled dusty and vinegary. I felt terribly alone. I poked the little trap door, and a friendly red face peered down at me.

"Wot you want, dearie?"

"Nothing," I answered, far too embarrassed to tell him that I was suddenly quite scared, all alone in a hansom cab in London with my future so close upon me, and needed to see a kindly face.

"Yer almost home," he comforted me. "Want a bull's-eye, missy?" He handed down a heavenly sweet marblelike candy. It had a black center which peered out of its glassy brown sugar coating like a human eyeball. I popped it into my mouth and sucked it happily, sweet streamers of molasses peppermint comforting me. The cabbie didn't close the trap again. He must have known I needed his comforting presence.

At the Carlton Mansions he cranked the door back with a proper gesture and climbed stiffly down to help me out. This was indeed an honor, one usually reserved for beautiful ladies in feathered hats and voluminous skirts.

"Good luck to you, little missy." He beamed on me.

"Oh, thank you." I could have hugged him, but I tried to convey my gratitude with a smile.

Upstairs Mother was still in bed. "I'm so discouraged," she said, wiping a tear away. "I just don't feel up to going down to dinner. I dressed, but I felt so miserable, I had to go back to bed. At this rate, I'll be carried on board ship, and we haven't done a thing about your audition. I must speak to Mr. MacGregor. He'll surely be able to arrange something for you, but I wanted to do it all myself."

"I know," I said. "Don't worry, Mom. Lie back in bed and I'll put some cold cloths on your head." Later that night I called Mr. MacGregor. He was out of town. I called the nurse. She came back, wrapped Mother in cold sheets again, and gave her a pill. I knew Mother wanted to be home with my father more than anything in the world. I cried myself to sleep. I wanted my father, too. I was lonely and homesick. I was so worried about Mother that I had ceased entirely to worry about my audition, though deep in my heart I knew I was going to the Gaiety the next morning if Mother was well enough to be left.

chapter 4:   The Audition

I HEARD the door of our room open softly the next morning.
Then I saw the nurse in her little brown toque and street coat.
She smiled, her finger on her lip. "Your mother's asleep,
dearie. I'll go after the tea. Lie back and rest yourself. It's
that foggy out, you'd best stay home today. Nothing's stir-
ring."

"Fog?" I'd heard about London fogs, but I'd never seen
one. I hurried to the window, pulled up the shades, and
though the window was open, I was greeted by a soft sponge-
like cloud obscuring everything except the looming ghostly
shapes of nearby trees. Yellow, soft, almost a visible presence,
this queer foglike veil.

"Does it last long?" I asked, shivering as I dove back into
bed and accepted my hot tea a few moments later.

"Days, hours. Who knows?" she said vaguely. "Don't

practice till later, dearie. Your mother needs her rest." I nodded. That meant I was not to go leaping and flying about the sitting room in what were my setting-up exercises, a sadly distorted Dalcroze sort of garbled motion I had dreamed up from years of Dalcroze training and two weeks of Russian Ballet performances.

I dressed, ate a little breakfast, neither exclaiming over my favorite finnan haddie nor the fact that my toast was brought in hot and buttery instead of standing cold and forlorn in the little toast stand. I answered kindly inquiries briefly. "Yes, I can see there is no chance of a cab." Everything that moved merely crept along in slow motion. People leaving the house vanished in the mist at the foot of the steps and swam away in vague outlines. How could I ever get to the Gaiety? I really must. Today was Friday. The weekend was coming up. Monday we would be packing. We would sail Tuesday. I nearly wept at the horrid murk which kept me from my business. It was the voice of the young Australian woman speaking to her husband which penetrated my own fog. "I tell you, I am going to Selfridge's. Of course I can find it. The others have gone to classes and business. You're going to the museum, why shouldn't I go to the store?"

"May I go with you to the bus stop?" I asked. If we could find the bus stop, the bus would find the Gaiety for me.

"Sure thing," she told me. "Get your hat. I'll wait." Never before had I loved her as I did now. Graceful, tall, with violet eyes and taffy-colored hair, always dressed in bright colors, she, a bride of only a few months, had taken time to visit with Mother, take me to the museum where her husband was doing special research on Egypt, and invariably seen that I had a delicious, hearty tea.

In my room I bade Mother good morning, and explained that I would be leaving the house with Mrs. Dongan, whom I knew Mother liked immensely. "She's going to Selfridge's for some shopping," I added, knowing full well that it sounded as if I planned to shop with her.

"Have a nice time," Mother said, but her eyes closed as she spoke. "I'll ask Mr. MacGregor . . ." The nurse motioned me away. I picked up my brown paper package. It contained the elf costume which I had worn at Dana Hall, a home-made affair of white cheesecloth trimmed with Christmas tree tinsel. I had no lovely spray of apple blossoms to wave such as we'd had at school, and had compromised on a stalk of lilies. It didn't look quite right to me, being rather stiff, for the three lilies were spaced to make a perfect trident. However, it was the only species of artificial flower I had been able to find in the corner stationery store, and because it was quite fly-specked, the woman had let me have it for threepence.

"Ready, dear?" Mrs. Dongan asked, and I nodded. I held her arm tightly, but found that the fog was not an impenetrable one nor a "pea-souper." By peering hard, we could see about ten feet ahead of us, and by feeling carefully with our feet, we didn't topple off curbs. The street crossings were eerie and full of terrifying moving shadows. The clop-clop of horses' hoofs was slowed, buses had shining eyes and drove slowly like majestic dragons trailing sheets of mist.

"It's getting better," Mrs. Dongan said, then gave a scream and clutched me as a horse's hot breath panted in our faces. Shrinking back, I felt as if his big body, rattling harness, and rubber-tired carriage would grind us to pieces. "That was a near miss," a bobby told us. "Come along now, ladies, and look sharp."

"Thank you ever so," I said gratefully, realizing that it was his rough jerk backward on my shoulder that doubtless had saved us both from some very severe bruises.

"Worse than I thought," Mrs. Dongan said nervously.

"Hadn't you better come with me instead of going to the Monds'? I doubt they'll expect you on a day like this, and I feel awfully responsible, taking you out in such sticky weather."

"I'll get along," I explained. "I'm meeting someone." I crossed my fingers. I told myself it wasn't really a fib, for I certainly hoped I was meeting Mr. Stuart, Mr. Boucher, and Mr. Edwardes! But what if this frightful fog had prevented a rehearsal? I almost wept at the idea.

"All right then, dearie," she assured me, and boarded the panting monster waiting at the curb. It heaved and hiccuped and belched in the mist like something human. When it went away, I joined the next queue. "I want to go to the Gaiety Theatre, in the Strand," I explained.

"Take a ——," the conductor said, and I was pushed off the bus in the very faces of mounting passengers.

I couldn't see the numbers on the buses, and as I hadn't been able to understand the number he had shouted so glibly, I climbed aboard each one and timidly asked for the Gaiety. The third time I was pushed inside instead of off onto the sidewalk. Nervously I peered out, but I could see only phantom shapes moving slowly. The streets the conductor announced refused to turn into intelligible places in my worried brain.

"Where you going, dearie?" the woman beside me asked. "You're that squirmy, you're making me nervous."

"The Gaiety Theatre," I said. "I've never been there, and I don't know where to get off. Do you?"

"That I do," she said heavily. "I'm in a shop nearby for twenty long years and have never yet missed the stop. Settle down now like a little lidy while I have me a snooze. It'll be a good 'alf 'our yet before this crayture lands us there."

"All right," I agreed, and wriggled back into the seat and sat as stiffly still as I possibly could. I did peer this way and that, but I did my best not to wiggle and slide off the slippery straw seat. The woman dozed, snored softly, and dropped her chin on her chest. The red rose on her hat quivered with her breathing, but it proved she was alive; and anyway, if she'd never missed the stop in twenty years' traveling, it seemed unlikely that she'd miss it today, though I did keep a troubled eye on her to see she didn't go sound asleep.

She woke suddenly just as I was beginning to relax. She bounded to her feet, snatched her string bag from the floor, scrambled over me, then remembered me and caught me by the wrist. "Come along now," she scolded, and hauled me after her down the aisle and down the steps.

"It's clearing a bit," she said, moving her head from side to side like a clock pendulum. "There 'tis." She motioned to a shadowy bulk. "The Gaiety," she explained. "Good luck, dearie. I'm on my way." And before I could say thank you, she darted off. Alone, and feeling quite lost in the murk, the noise of unseen traffic in my ears, I joined a cluster of strangers and let myself be carried across the street, hoping for the best and fearing the worst. On the other side of the street everyone evaporated. Apparently everyone but I knew where he was going. I peered this way and that. Certainly the Gaiety's stage entrance would not have swing-doors or a bar. Finally I stumbled into a doorway where a man sat all hunched down, reading a newspaper.

"'Allo there. Wot you got?" He eyed my package.

"For Mr. Stuart or Mr. Boucher. I have to give it to one of them myself." I clutched the package fiercely. It was quite evident that the doorman took me for an errand girl, and something told me I was very much in luck. He looked like the kind of man whose *no* would be insurmountable.

"Yer don't sye." He peered at me over his glasses and I peered back without glasses as fearsomely as I could. He made a move to snatch the package, and I gave a little growl.

"Ow, now!" His rasp was half laugh. "Go on in and give it yerself, if yer that set on a tip."

I hurried into the theater, realizing for the first time that in my haste to leave, I hadn't dressed properly at all, and was wearing an old pleated skirt, a white middy blouse, a shabby red sweater, and a tam much the worse for being snatched off, thrown on the ground, and stepped on.

Inside the theater I found myself in a maze of doors. It smelled moldy and was quite dark. The electric lights were dim and did little to help me find my way. I tried several different paths and had gone only a few feet when I met a closed door. The third one led me on stage, and I was suddenly out in a huge empty space, whose shadows were brilliantly lit in one spot by a huge electric bulb with a tin protector. The footlights were dark. The house was huge, cavernous, and empty, its seats under dust covers. The boxes were vacant and forlorn, but my attention was riveted on three men sitting on three kitchen chairs. Motionless, like figures at Mme. Tussaud's Waxwork Exhibition, they seemed less real people than dummies.

Finally one figure moved. Languidly it picked a bottle of beer from the floor, drank from it, unwrapped a bulky sandwich. "That for me?" it asked, pointing to my package.

"No, it's mine," I said breathlessly. "It's my costume. I came to dance for you."

"Huh!" said one.

"How'd you get in?" asked another wearily.

"A new trick," sighed the third.

"You American?" asked number one.

I burst into speech. I explained how I'd come to London to see the Queen, or anyway seeing the Queen was an excuse for coming to London. That I wanted to dance and that unless they saw me and said I was quite good, I'd have to go back to America and never dance again, just live a horrid respectable life.

"You mean there's no dancing in America?" Number two asked.

"I don't know," I said quite honestly. "I saw Adeline Genée, but she came back here. Karsavina and Nijinsky are here. Pavlova's here. Of course, I haven't seen her," I said honestly, "but I'm going to. Tonight," I added, for it was tonight that Mr. MacGregor had invited Mother and me to go to the Palace as his guests. It was our farewell party, and I meant to go unless Mother was really and truly breathing her last.

"You don't say." Number one was looking at me very hard.

"Why don't we let the kid dance?" he asked.

I didn't wait for an answer from the others. "I'll change back here," I explained, and darted behind a flat. I emerged in costume, carrying my lily, for all the world like a character in a Gilbert and Sullivan operetta. A muffled gurgle I took for praise encouraged me.

"What will you dance?" A figure disengaged itself from a chair and strolled to a piano.

"It doesn't matter," I said grandly. "I can dance to anything you play. That is, if you can play." I didn't mean to be rude, but because he moved so aimlessly and put no music on the stand, I began to have my doubts.

"I can play well enough," he told me, and there was assurance not only in the tone of his voice but in the way his fingers found the keys and drew melody from them. I listened for a few bars, then began to dance. Rhythm had been my love since early childhood, movement to music was dancing to me. My body and my spirit, it seemed, were one. The notes spoke to me and I moved with them, hand in hand, note for step. The man at the piano was half turned, watching me. Sometimes I could see his face. The music changed pace, was fast, slow, choppy, beautifully languid, then suddenly lilting and gay. Happily for me, we ended simultaneously, he on a chord, I in my very best low bow.

Shyly I looked up.

"Not bad," said one.

"She could be taught to dance," the second agreed.

"A good sense of rhythm," the man at the piano spoke with authority.

"Do you think I have talent? That I can succeed as a dancer?" I was standing beside the man at the piano. I was sure he was my man.

"I wouldn't go so far as to say you'll succeed," he said cautiously, "but you might. You'll have to work very hard for two or three years. Music hall, vaudeville, musical comedy, pantomime, of course," he added. "You'll never make a Giselle."

"I know," I said, "but you think I could dance quite nicely?"

"Yes, I do," he said suddenly. "It's a hunch. You go along with me?" he asked the other two men. They nodded.

I stared, and somehow I felt let down instead of elated. I'd had my audition, I had been told I might succeed, but what next? Two or three years' study in England before my debut? Utterly impossible, I knew. We had enough money to live on, to pay our bills and stretch out to modest schooling, but years of study abroad—oh, no! I didn't know what to say. Such an explanation not only was out of character, but was so deadly dull.

I choked. I wept a dramatic unreluctant tear. "I'm an orphan," I sobbed. "I'd have to have a scholarship. I couldn't pay for all those lessons and things. Oh, dear!"

People were arriving on stage. Someone sat down at the

piano and began to strum. Girls in leotards and tutus began doing *barre* exercises. Two began to waltz together. A group lined up and began kicking. The lights came on. My three men sat up straight and looked interested.

"Stop blubbering and come see me this afternoon at four-thirty. I expect I can get you some lessons practically free," the man who had played for me said, smiling, handing me a card. "Cut along now, girlie, we're busy."

I dressed in a daze. I walked out into the sunshine, stopped only by the doorman's thunderous, "Wot you doing with that there parcel?"

"It's my costume," I said, dangling it on its string. "I've just had an audition. I'm going to be a dancer."

What he said won't bear repeating. I hailed a hansom and drove home in state, though I had to keep the driver waiting while I rushed in for change to pay him with. Somehow I'd mislaid my purse.

It was lunchtime. Mother was motionless in bed, quite covered with a wet sheet. Only her face was visible. Her eyes were shut. The nurse was downstairs getting her lunch. I tiptoed in and whispered, "Mother, it's all right. You can go on home to Father when the boat sails. Mr. Leslie Stuart saw me dance this morning and he says I have talent and that he'll get me some lessons practically free. I can stay here in London and learn how to dance and it won't cost you and Father a single cent."

"What's that you say?" Mother opened her eyes wide. She rose from her bed in one lithe motion. She swept about the bedroom and the sitting room waving her arms, which, as she still wore the sheets, made her look exactly like Loie Fuller without the lights. Mother was still talking, asking questions and quarreling with my answers, when the nurse arrived with her tray.

"Why, Mrs. Jones," she said helplessly as Mother pirouetted before her, waving her draperies in angry swirls. "You should be in bed."

"In bed!" Mother snorted. "Me, in bed, with this naughty child going for auditions and saying she's an orphan and arranging to stay in London for goodness knows how long all by herself! Bed indeed! I'm quite well. I'm getting up and getting dressed. I'll be going to see this Leslie Stuart with her myself this afternoon and find out what's going on. What's there for lunch?" Mother sniffed the tray accusingly. "I couldn't bear another poached egg," she decided. "You eat it, nurse, and then I'll pay you. I'm going downstairs for lunch. I need some good nourishing food after a shock like this. Wash your hands and comb your hair, Regina. You look a sight. I suppose you're hungry, too?"

I was, and we enjoyed our lunch immensely. I never before knew that cold shoulder of mutton and fruit and custard could taste so delicious.

At four-thirty Mother and I rang the doorbell of Mr. Stuart's big house on Russell Square. Mother wore her best black taffeta suit, which she had embroidered most beautifully, and a huge purple velvet hat with a willow plume, one which dripped off and down onto her shoulder. I was dressed in my blue changeable taffeta coat, all hand-smocked. My bonnet was the last word in magnificence. It was made of the same blue taffeta as my coat. It had a wide frill wired stiffly, which made it stand up all around my face. It was lined with pleated white chiffon, and around the hairline were adorable pink moss-rose buds and tiny green velvet leaves. My dress was white Liberty silk, and I wore white silk socks and black patent strap slippers. I must have looked exactly like an oversized, overdressed French doll.

Seated in the huge drawing room, Mother and I waited stiffly. I could see the curving staircase up which the man-servant went and down which Mr. Stuart descended. As he came toward us, he looked at us curiously, his eyes moving from Mother to me and back to her. He did not need to be told anything. He went directly to her and took her hand. He was smiling.

"She's a terrible little liar," he admitted, "but she really can dance."

It broke the horrible tension of explanation and apologies. In five minutes Mr. Stuart had promised introductions to various teachers. "It'll be all right," he said vaguely. "Won't cost you much. Maybe a pound a week for each. See how she makes out. I can get her in at Drury Lane. Young D'Auban, I suppose. Old man doesn't take any new pupils. Zanfretta, of course." Mr. Stuart was writing on his card. "Show this," he said, giving it to me. "It'll get you a real discount. Come back in six months or a year. If you need anything, just give me a ring. Poor little orphan!" he added, as he pinched my cheek, his eyes on Mother's diamonds and my elegant coat. We shook hands good-by, smiling.

"As easy as that," Mother said. "Well, I'll just cable your father. Then I'll cancel our passage and arrange for our rooms by the month. Thank goodness for Grandma's money. It will take care of everything for at least a year."

"You mean we're going to s-stay," I stammered. "That you're g-going to stay, too?"

"Of course," Mother said calmly. "Your father and I said you should have your chance if you had talent, and Mr. Stuart says he thinks you have. What else can we do?"

"I don't know," I said, quite dazed by all that was happening. "I just can't believe it. You mean we're going to live in London and that I'm going to study dancing?"

"You certainly are," Mother said. "We'll go see Mr. D'Auban and Zanfretta tomorrow. I'll go to the museums while you go to your lessons. I think I'll take up my painting again."

We walked toward Carlton Mansions in silence. How strange, how very strange, to have a dream come true and suddenly be starting to live it in such an ordinary everyday way. London, the stage, a career as a dancer ahead . . . and all because clutched in the palm of my hand was a white visiting card bearing the magic name *Leslie Stuart* and the words, "I think this child has talent, do what you can for her." Leslie Stuart, the composer of *Floradora,* the man to whom I had said, ". . . if you can play . . ." when he sat at the piano.

"Let's celebrate," Mother said suddenly. "Tea at Rumpel-mayers. Then on to the American Express. There's really no hurry about cabling if we're going to stay on for a couple of years, Is there?"

I shook my head. It didn't seem possible that this could be happening to me. It was just too, too wonderful to be true.

chapter 5:   *Pavlova and Mordkin*

WE DIDN'T HAVE tea at Rumpelmayers at all. We fell from grace with a dull thud and had delicious cups of hot chocolate foaming over with yellow whipped cream, tiny fancy sandwiches, and delectable pastries iced in heavenly pastels. Amethyst icing was violet flavored, pearl-pink tasted of roses, emerald-green, of pistachio. It was the first time I'd ever seen sugared flowers. The lavender cakes were graced with real violets, candied in a rough sweet coating. The pink icing was decorated with real rose petals, curly and sugared. Here we saw and smelled our first perfumed cigarettes. Unbelievable to us, to see ladies puffing clouds of sweet-smelling smoke from pink and yellow cigarettes. The curious cloying odors made us feel ill and drove us out finally, forcing us to leave our delicate pastries and chocolate unfinished.

"Horrible!" Mother gulped mouthfuls of fresh moist air

in annoyance. "Smoking like chimneys nasty stuff that smells like a hothouse on fire. I prefer the tobacco smell of the good strong cigars your father smokes. That place is too rich for my blood. We'll have tea at Lyons' hereafter. Let's walk home."

We trudged along, and suddenly I remembered. "Mother! Tonight Mr. MacGregor is taking us to see Pavlova. Are you well enough to go?" I stopped dead on the sidewalk. Homecoming pedestrians parted considerately and walked around us.

"Pavlova! Tonight? Stop that hansom!" Mother waved her ever-present umbrella at a cabby, and the horse's head turned toward us. Big liquid eyes peered into our own a moment, then the hansom drew up alongside the curb. We climbed in. "Leave the doors open, please," Mother requested. "I like riding in this contraption," she told me, "but I do not want to be sealed up in it like a half-canned sardine."

The horse's rump moved up and down, his ears perked this way and that, the cabby's voice droned on as he pointed out the sights.

"He knows we're trippers," Mother said. "How long do you suppose it'll be before we get over it and look like Londoners?"

"Maybe a year," I hazarded. But it was sooner than that when we could fool American tourists with our knowledge of London town and our British accent. But we never fooled an Englishman nor an Englishwoman for a single minute.

We were so busy recounting my triumph at the Gaiety that we had no time to eat our dinner. Dressing took no time at all, for we were both much too excited to care how we looked. We were going to see Pavlova, not to be seen.

Mr. MacGregor had not arrived, but Mr. Alfred Butt, manager of the theater, was waiting, and escorted us to his

61

box on the orchestra floor on the right side of the auditorium. The vaudeville turns were very good, the humor, very English, the pace, medium fast, but I sat tensely, waiting, waiting for the curtain to go up on Pavlova and Mordkin.

When it did, I saw not the famed crystal beauty of a classic ballerina in white tutu and blocked toe shoes. Instead there romped on stage a gamin elf, in silken rags, purple grapes in great clusters twined in her dark loose curls. Mordkin, beside her, was virile, stalwart, and a being worthy of her wanton charm. With flying scarf, leaps, bounds, pirouettes, and fancy lifts and falls, the pair quite took my breath away. Technically I saw nothing, for I knew nothing, but dancing such as this was an exciting, uplifting, moving experience.

"She's wonderful, just wonderful," I babbled. As Pavlova bowed, I wondered when I might once again see the swaying leaflike movement. It was as if her body were being blown about by a gentle breeze that tossed her here and there in playful jest. In her *L'Automme Bacchanale* her eyes smoldered, her face lit in the gayest of smiles, her teeth sparkled, her lips curved enticingly. And then, suddenly, her lovely face grew sullen, dark, cruel. No matter what role Pavlova essayed, there was always a magical luminous quality about her interpretation which riveted one's attention. Even years later I felt that spell. When I understood technique, when I had studied ballet myself, when I had seen dozens of great ballerinas and was able to compare one with the other, it seemed that only Pavlova had that tantalizing ability to command total attention. When she was dancing, the stage was hers alone. What the corps did, what her partner did, seemed of no moment. Even when she herself danced, you were apt to find yourself enchanted with her as a person rather than with the steps she was doing.

The Dying Swan was a delicate trill-like bit of *pointe* work, mostly *bourrées*, which Pavlova did faster than I've ever seen them done. Indeed, that dance as done now is less like Pavlova's than would seem possible. Her *bourrées* sizzled. They were quick as a pecking bird's beak, and there was never a glint of light between the swiftly moving feet, where now there are six inches. Pavlova moved on two *pointes*, but they always looked like one. She poised, she fairly flew; her feathers shivered, her arms quivered. She didn't plod, shake, undulate, as her copyists do. She was the soul of the dying swan, while her imitators are but clumsy humans in swans' feathers.

Gliding about the stage, stumbling, life slipping away in convulsive breaths, Pavlova was truly a dying bird-woman. The sudden rigidity of her death pose, one leg bent at the knee, the other straight out, head bowed over it, arms crossed on the ankle, was almost too beautiful to bear. It always brought a sudden, almost audible silence. Then came the applause. Quick, hard, enthusiastic. Mme. Pavlova rose and bowed. She smiled over at our box, but though I basked in it, the smile was for Mr. Butt and Mr. MacGregor.

"Shall we go backstage and meet her?" Mr. MacGregor asked, and I nodded mutely. He handed me a bunch of violets with one red rose in the center. He had removed the wrappings. "For you to give Madame," he told me, and I nodded my thanks. Mother and I followed him backstage, through the wings, behind the curtain. There were people onstage, a tight wire, acrobats in creamy tights and spangles. I heard applause and laughter, but I did not look back.

The rap on the door elicited a quick *"Entrez,"* and in we went. Madame was out of the feathered tutu and in a pale pink cotton kimono. She still wore the winged headdress and had not yet creamed her face. She gave Mr. Mac-

Gregor her hand. He introduced Mother, then me. I bobbed a curtsy. It had been years since I had made one, but it seemed in place here.

Pavlova smiled. She sniffed the rose. She looked straight at me as Mr. MacGregor told her I had been auditioned and seemed to have talent.

"So, you wish to dance." The big eyes narrowed, the sweet mouth firmed, there was a perceptible chilling of her charm, as if she questioned my right to approach her art.

"Yes," I said in a very small voice. "Not in opera ballets of course, just music hall."

"This is a music hall," she reminded me.

"It is more than that when you dance," I answered boldly. "It is like the Covent Garden performance. You are the most beautiful dancer I have ever seen."

"Indeed? Which dance do you prefer that I did tonight?"

"The *Bacchanale*. That is the way I would like to dance."

She looked at me quizzically. "Then dancing is not all the fluffy white tutu?"

I shook my head. "No, it's pretty, but I like it best when you dance around the stage so wildly and get so angry you look as if you could bite Mr. Mordkin."

Pavlova gave a little throaty laugh. "Come again, come often and watch me, and I will be very angry, right at your side of the stage. Perhaps someday I will really bite Mr. Mordkin. Now run along. I am very tired."

"You did very well," Mr. MacGregor told me. "Madame's always polite, but she talked longer to you than to most young hopefuls. By the way, I have the use of that box. Come in any or every night as long as you please. It's empty most of the time, though I do try to drop in and catch a glimpse of her when it's possible."

"Thank you," I said, and I meant it. Mother and I went

64

almost every night of Pavlova's engagement at the Palace. We arrived before she came on stage and left when she had taken her last bow. The nights that are fixed in my memory are the occasional ones when she took her flowers and her bows near our box. Sometimes she would toss me a rose from a basket she held, and I would catch it and hold it to my cheek and take it home and press it as a good luck token. But it was the brilliant smile, the recognition in her eyes, that meant the most to me. I was there, and Pavlova knew it. I asked nothing more.

That first night, though, it was as if a whole new field of dancing had opened up with my seeing the *Bacchanale*. No longer was dancing merely a matter of filmy skirts and flowered heads. Now it was a more earthy, more human, kind of movement. Dramatic dancing, of which I had never before heard, had become reality, and my love for it has never wavered for one moment.

I slept and dreamed and woke to a cold rainy day and the necessity for enrolling as a student at Drury Lane and at Mme. Zanfretta's. Suddenly the future loomed ahead, a vista of chilling commonplaces. Breakfast, buses, classes, new faces, new steps, new ideas. By the time I had arrived at Drury Lane, I was a mass of nerves. I stammered when I met Mr. D'Auban the Younger. If it had not been for Mr. Stuart's card, which Mr. D'Auban twiddled between his fingers, I realized I would never have been accepted as a pupil.

"You can try this morning class," he said finally. "You may not care for it. If not, you can drop out."

I realized he was giving me, an American, a graceful out at the end of the week's lessons. I determined to stay in class as long as he would let me, even though what he was teaching seemed to have nothing at all to do with the kind of dancing I had seen Pavlova do.

Mother and I ate lunch at a Lyons restaurant. I was not hungry, and merely tore my currant bun apart and sipped my lukewarm tea.

At Mme. Zanfretta's I found a brisk heavy-set woman with an oily complexion and a very heavy topknot of dark hair. She was wearing a Roman-striped silk blouse and a long wide black broadcloth skirt looped up on one side like a riding habit. She was unimpressed by my appearance and Mr. Stuart's card. She flicked it onto a table, told me to change into practice clothes, snorted indignantly at sight of my bloomers and middy blouse, and handed Mother a sheet of yellow paper with the name of a place to buy slippers and a leotard.

I worked out at a *barre*, and Mother, the linguist of the family, reported that Madame said, "My God, *pas possible!*" in horrified tones in a dozen different languages, all progressively more profoundly shocked.

In heavily accented English, and emphasizing each word with a wicked whack of her cane, she told me,"You do not know wan zingle zing about ze ballet. You are terreebal! You mak me to shivair. I do not know eef I can stand to watch you, but I try. I try! Kom bak tomorrow weeth decent costume two o'clock. Good-by." She looked away and shuddered.

"Well!" Mother snorted as I dressed slowly. "This does not seem to be very hopeful, does it? Mr. D'Auban didn't like your dancing and Madame is horrified by it."

"I know." I wiped away a couple of tears running down my nose. "I guess the truth is I *am* terrible. I like dancing, but I don't know any more about it than a cab horse. I'm going to learn though. I'm going to show them."

"What?" Mother asked practically. "Who?" I didn't answer because I didn't know.

For a week Mother went with me to classes. Then she

66

rebelled. "These lessons bore me to tears. I hate the way those teachers spit commands at you. They're so mean, I could spit back. I believe I'll just go to the art galleries and sketch while you have your lessons. I don't want to learn to dance," she added, as if in apology.

"That's all right," I agreed. "I can go by myself. I know the way."

"Are you really very lame?" Mother asked as I limped along beside her. I nodded. She turned in to a Boots chemist shop and asked for liniment. "I wish I'd brought some of Aunty Barb's," she told me. "It's wonderful. I'll write her and ask her to send us a couple of bottles."

"My daughter is studying ballet," Mother told the clerk. "She's so lame in the mornings she can hardly move. Do you have a good liniment?"

"Oh, yes, Madame." He smiled politely, and brought out a bottle of creamy liquid. "Elliman's Horse Liniment. It'll make a new girl out of her."

"Good thing if it made a new dancer," Mother muttered. "She's all legs and elbows. An absolute gawk. She used to be very graceful. Now she looks like a drunken camel."

"That's always the way when you're learning anything new," the man said kindly as he wrapped and tied the bottle, making a neat loop to slip over the finger. "Get worse before you get better, you know. Darkest before dawn and all that."

Mother nodded.

That night she rubbed me for twenty minutes. Elliman's liniment had the most horrible barnlike smell imaginable, but it was greasy and soothing. Mother sniffed in disgust, but for the first time in weeks I fell asleep without crying over my several hundred protesting muscles.

The following morning I even managed to creep downstairs holding onto the banisters instead of sitting down and bumping down each step on my behind. Elliman's was a success. Everyone at the table congratulated me on the achievement.

Mother became concerned about my formal education about this time, and a governess was hired to come in each evening between seven and nine o'clock. Afterward we would drive to the Palace, see Pavlova dance, and return immediately. A hot bath costing a shilling, a rubdown with Elliman's Horse Liniment, and bed. The days were taken up with my lessons with Mr. D'Auban at Drury Lane and a lesson from one to three at Zanfretta's. I would then meet Mother and spend a couple of hours in some museum, for Mother felt that seeing great paintings and sculptures would help me be a better dancer. She was very systematic. She would sketch any pose that interested me, and at home I would attempt to place myself in these poses. While I did this Mother was interested and helpful. However, the moment I began the acrobatic exercises Mr. D'Auban was teaching me, she would snatch her long woolly scarf, pick up her embroidery, and hasten out of the room to sit downstairs in the public living room until I had finished. Every evening she would say the same thing quite plaintively as I started my back bends.

"Dear me." She would shake her head nervously. "Do you really have to turn yourself inside out to learn to dance?" Then, without waiting for my answer, she would open the door and disappear, leaving me to do back bends and to try to remember dates for my history lesson at one and the same time. Always Mother's last words would ring in my ears: "I simply cannot bear to watch you. I do *not* believe any dancing is worth so much effort!" I myself never questioned the value of the exercises. I was a docile pupil. I admired my teachers. I wanted to learn to dance. Therefore I did exactly as I was told, and loved it.

chapter 6: *Westminster Abbey and Tea at Selfridge's*

SUNDAY WAS my mother's favorite day. She loved churches, and all the churches were lit up, filled with people and music, sermons and prayers. It was also the day she could insist on my doing something besides dance. She reasoned that everyone needed a change of pace and that the Good Lord knew exactly what He was doing when He planned one day of rest out of seven.

Mother wasn't above interpreting the word "rest" to suit herself. For us, *rest* was not defined as "repose." *Rest* meant doing something other than our regular daily round, something which was rewarding mentally and spiritually. Where better find this, my mother reasoned, than in the busy churches and small art collections? Church architecture was my mother's passion. Stained glass was a close second, and music made a very good third. So, to churches we went. Not to one church but to two, three, or four, depending entirely on how much time was spent in art galleries.

"But, Mother, I have to practice," I insisted. "Dancers can't let a single day go by without practicing."

"Very well. Practice as much as you like," Mother agreed blithely, "but you must be dressed and ready to go to Westminster for the ten o'clock service. Just be ready at nine-fifteen, dear."

"But when can I practice? Breakfast is at eight-thirty."

"Beforehand, my dear. Get up at six. That'll give you two hours."

"Mother! Everyone sleeps late on Sunday."

Mother's look was as innocent as a kitten's whose mustache still glistens from lapping stolen cream. "Oh, well, if you prefer sleeping to dancing . . ." She left the question up in the air. Of course, I got up and practiced. There was no other time in the day to do so.

Westminster Abbey was a must. No matter how many Sundays we promised ourselves we would go elsewhere, ten o'clock saw us well up in front in the gloriously somber, gloriously designed Abbey. The service itself seemed more deeply moving, the music more thunderous and more likely to penetrate heavenly space than that of any other church. Even the sermons satisfied us, and we seldom left without roaming about the church by ourselves or taking guided tours till we were greeted as old friends by the guides. We knew what they would say as well as they did.

"Westminster Abbey, the Abbey of St. Peter, is the most widely celebrated church in the British Empire.

"It is cruciform in shape.

"Construction was started in 1050 by Edward the Confessor.

"Every sovereign from William the Conqueror on except for Edward V has been crowned in the Abbey.

"The Stone of Scone is beneath the coronation chair in the Confessor's Chapel.

"A great many famous people are buried here, also a great many not so famous. There are also monuments to many important people who are not buried here."

We never tired of listening. We always learned something new and interesting or saw something we had not seen before. Westminster Abbey is as much a part of my London year as Pavlova, Genée, my teachers, or London fog.

After dinner everyone else went up for naps. We went up for our hats. Then, unless we were being taken out for a drive, we headed straight for an art museum. Mother detested walking. I really believe she thought walking was something for horses. Nevertheless, as we could not hire a hack to take us through museums, Mother forgot her prejudice and walked as steadily as any bobby on his beat. I tired. I fidgeted. My feet hurt. My legs ached. I went and sat down. But Mother was indefatigable, and before long I was on my feet again and marching slowly and methodically through acres of picture galleries. I soon learned to enjoy them, though never with the assurance of my mother. I loved line, form, and color. My Mother loved every brush stroke, and was as reverent before a Rembrandt or a Rubens as I would have been if faced with Karsavina and Nijinsky doing a duet for me alone.

After evensong at any church which happened to be near the museum we were visiting, we went on to supper with friends, or home to a cold buffet at Carleton Mansions. Mother usually visited downstairs while I spent half an hour at the piano. It had become evident to us that a knowledge of music was quite as necessary to a dancer as lessons or practice. A rented piano appeared, and the little governess who taught history and mathematics was replaced by an accompanist, for though I was a docile pupil when with my teachers, I was anything but the instant I was away from them.

I had had a fairly good musical education as a child, and was quite prepared to choose my own music and make my dances to it. I had never heard of the word "choreography," but I created my own dances long before I had ever had a proper lesson, and continued to do so the rest of my professional life.

I must have been what the French call an *originale*, for though my teachers wrung their hands, pulled long faces, and scolded me volubly in class, never once did a single one laugh at me or tell me to stop trying to work out my own dances. It was nearly two years later that M. Leo Staats, ballet master of the Paris Opera, smiled at me in farewell and sent me off to audition as a professional, with the words, "You dance very well indeed. From now on you will dance better if you dance your own way. I think you are ready to forget the rules and dance as you please."

If the truth were told, I always had. Not that I hadn't tried my very best to do what my teachers told me to do. At each lesson I had worked seriously and with all my physical abilities to follow my teacher's instructions; and yet, I had hardly reached home, gobbled my tea, and changed into the despised middy and bloomers than I was at it again, though now I was "creating" with a vengeance. I knew what I wanted of my body. I knew what kind of dancing, what kind of music, what the dance should look like, and what I wanted to say.

It was a long, long time ago that a little American girl worked madly in a big sitting room in a pension in Bedford Place, but it was in that room that I became a dancer, for there I was myself and I danced as I pleased. I needed every lesson I took, and I'm grateful for them and for the patience of the teachers who put up with me. How out of step I was with the hundreds of girls with whom I practiced only they and I ever knew, and yet my teachers let me keep on. They it was who let me study, mature, and grow entirely at my own rate as I literally sweated it out. Thanks to their blandly unseeing eyes, I remained in one studio or the other from the moment it opened until it closed. I was at Drury Lane at eight-thirty and ate my lunch on the landing of the back stairs until the day Mr. D'Auban the Elder found me doing so. From then on we ate our lunches together in his crowded little office, where he directed my mind toward the great dancers of the past, showed me programs and clippings, yellowed and dusty, and told me thrilling tales of the great and the near great. Sometimes he would play snatches of ballet on his violin just for me. He was a consecrated teacher. At one o'clock I would say good-by to him and hurry off to my ballet class with Mme. Zanfretta.

No doubt that both my teachers knew, or at least suspected from the way I danced, that I took lessons elsewhere, but as this was the sin of sins, neither brought the matter up. This may have been because the truth would have been disconcerting and would have precipitated a crisis of some sort. As it was, I took everybody's lessons in each studio, class or private. Sometimes even, I was called on to demonstrate steps. How many private lessons of this sort I had each day I'll never know, but they no doubt were the explanation for my rapid progress.

I was too busy now to make daily trips to museums, but Saturday and Sunday Mother and I continued to study paintings and sculptures. We went each evening to the Palace until Mr. D'Auban the Elder insisted that good as Pavlova was, not to see Genée was sheer idiocy. So I gave in and went to the Empire where she was appearing in a ballet called *Butterflies and Roses*. It was an evening of sheer delight. Adeline Genée was a beautiful woman and a truly great ballerina. She had an enchanted quality which exactly fitted the Never-Never Land of the ballet's title. Genée looked exactly like a

French bisque doll, but she danced like an angel. While she had a meticulously perfect technique, every step was understated to avoid the commonplace spectacular. Where other dancers strained in an *arabesque* or an *attitude* after extensive preparation, Genée drifted from *arabesque* to *attitude* with the ease of a languid butterfly. In 1911 most dancers stabbed or glided or stumped about the stage in their *bourrées*. Not Genée. She seemed to float a little above it, as if disdaining gravity. One afternoon when Mr. D'Auban was talking to a group of ardent young balletomanes, he said, "I would bet a guinea that Adeline Genée is the only ballerina who could dance on a sheet of tissue paper without rumpling it." No one took his bet. We had seen Genée and knew he was betting on a sure thing.

Mr. D'Auban also insisted that I see Maude Allan and the Morris Dancers, pointing out that no matter what my preference was, there were other kinds of dance and dancers than my beloved ballet and Anna Pavlova. Indeed, by now, Pavlova was so well known to me that I needed only to close my eyes to have her dance again in filmy retrospect. Every step, movement, flashing smile and shaking curl was etched in my mind's eye. When I was terribly bored at concerts or ballets, I would summon Pavlova, and with my eyes tightly shut transport myself to a dancer's heaven as I reveled in her grace and beauty. Nowadays Pavlova is cherished for her fragility, her crystal-like clarity of line, but I cherish the innocent wanton, the wicked sprite of the *Bacchanale*, abandoned, richly lyric, utterly devastating in her passionately seductive techniques.

Lessons, formal ones, had vanished in the press of duties. There was so much to learn about dancing, and there was never enough time. I grudged the hours spent in museums, the visits to art galleries, the study of costume. Mother was determined. "If a dancer is not dressed to show off her movement to advantage, her dance can be quite spoiled. You may not choose to design your own costumes, but you must always be able to support your criticism of their defects by knowledge. You must be aware of the line of your costume in relation to your body and what you wish it to achieve." We spent days and days in such study, and I have been very grateful for it. It was never my fate to appear in a costume in which I could not dance or which ruined my motion. However, I tried many such on. But for my mother, I should surely have worn them in public.

I had been studying only two months, but already I felt as at home in London as if I had lived there all my life. Sundays had become routine. Westminster Abbey, dinner, a museum, St. Paul's for vesper service, and on to visit Mr. Dottridge, a friend of my father's in the Masonic Lodge. Mr. Dottridge had two sons at the university, and often they were present; but from the height of twenty-one and twenty-two, my mere fifteen years received no recognition. They were polite, they ate steak and kidney pie and jam tart with us, but after supper they excused themselves to go calling on proper young ladies or to retire to the library to study, while Mother, Mr. Dottridge, and I put on earphones and listened to the latest Gilbert and Sullivan, or, to my delight, Harry Lauder's hoarse gravelly voice, which was music to my ears.

In 1911, to be able to listen to shows as they were going on —"live," as we'd say now—was fantastic. That a mere remark to the operator such as, "Give me the Gaiety," could result in listening to the show going on there seemed a miracle. I never quite got over the novelty. At home in Boston, though we had a telephone and electric lights, we had no such exciting instrument as this, with headphone receivers which clamped onto our ears and which permitted us to be elsewhere in spirit. I usually sat bolt upright and motionless on the sofa, frozen in position, fearing that a sudden movement on my part would break the spell and end the music.

Soon after nine we had to leave. *Had* is perhaps a strong word, but that is what it amounted to. I insisted I must practice for an hour. Mother was quite agreeable. I could stay as long as I liked at Mr. Dottridge's listening to *Patience* or Harry Lauder's "I Love a Lassie." I could practice as much as I chose before going to bed—but I had to be in bed by ten-fifteen! Mother was adamant about that. "You need your beauty sleep more than most," she'd point out. "You are not even pretty, so the least you can do is look fresh and rested." I'd heard this often. Mother had often said quite dispassionately, "You'll have to be smart. No one will ever marry you for your looks."

One Wednesday afternoon Madame Zanfretta called off all her classes. The studio was being used for professional tryouts. I attempted to linger behind as usual, but was swept out with the rest of the students. We walked by the Empire and recognized Lydia Kyasht.

"It's a rehearsal for *Sylvia's* principals, I think," one of the other girls told me, and we stood on the sidewalk and watched the fabulously lovely Lydia Kyasht go in to practice. Another day I saw Adeline Genée on the street outside Madame Zanfretta's. The meeting depressed me. She was so exquisitely lovely; her dancing, I now knew, was a thing of utter perfection. Years of training, years of absolutely rigid technical attainment, a phenomenally lovely personality, and a flawless physique. Who was I, a clumsy, oaflike adolescent who would never, could never, even hope to approach the ability of such a one as she, to try to dance? I never thought of Pavlova, Karsavina, Kyasht, Lopokova, as people, for I'd only seen them dance or glimpsed them in costume. Comparisons were as impossible as comparing the Sphinx with a doorstop! But Adeline Genée—here she was, exquisitely groomed, wearing simple clothes, and about to work in our very studio. Suddenly I saw this could never happen to me. I was an upstart, a complete and stupid idiot. What was I doing, practicing with a hundred other girls of all shapes and sizes, steps that I could not do, steps I could not even remember, steps that when I did remember, I mangled!

Mother was out when I got home. I was staring out the window, feeling very sorry for myself, when a knock on our door announced callers. I hurried downstairs, and there were Henry and Eva Violet Mond in the parlor. Eva was holding a huge bunch of roses.

"For your poor dear mama," she told me.

Henry added pointedly, "You wrote you were going to stay on, but you never came back to tell us about it."

"Oh, sorry. I was so busy." Suddenly I was breathless with all there was to tell. As I gabbled, they learned I was free of lessons at the moment, that Mother was well and at a museum.

"We should celebrate," Henry said. "Come on. We'll let Edmonds drive us in the park while you talk. We were supposed to take your mother for a drive, but you'll do. Then we can go home for tea."

We piled into the car and I talked on, amidst unbelieving, "Did you nows!" and, "Really, that was absolutely stunning!"

At four-thirty we all felt hungry. "We'll have to go home," Henry said. "I haven't a bean. How about you, Vi?"

"Thrippence," Vi said. "Home it is."

"No!" I was struck with a thrilling idea. "Let's go to Selfridge's. Have you ever been there?" They shook their heads. "They serve American things. Let me give you an American kind of afternoon tea. A club sandwich and a soda."

No sooner said than Edmonds obligingly headed the car toward Selfridge's. In the airy dining room I was accorded the best service, for I was well remembered from the two or three days we had spent like visiting royalty as guests of the management. Our tea did indeed consist of monster toasted club sandwiches, so huge we were dumbfounded as to how to eat them.

"Can't get your mouth around," Henry said.

"No way to cut them." Vi shook her head. We had forks, but no knives. I myself would have asked, and said so, but Henry shook his head.

"It's our problem." He eyed the outrageously thick wedges made up of three large squares of toast jammed with slices of chicken, tomatoes, lettuce, bacon, and mayonnaise, slightly stunned. "Look. If we all eat it alike, no one will know we're stymied. Let's eat the top toast in our hands and the filling with a fork."

It seemed an intelligent solution and we did this, one and all together as if this were the usual procedure. To our shocked surprise a very large, very American couple sitting at a nearby table laid hold of their club sandwiches and by main force squashed them together, forced open their mouths, and ate them in large bites. We continued our way, feeling very virtuous in our less conspicuous manner of eating.

The sodas were less of a success than anticipated. The ice cream was very hard and bobbed disconcertingly about. Vi had a vanilla soda, Henry, a strawberry; mine was chocolate. We sampled each other's through straws, and were as polite as possible about the taste, but they all did seem impossibly sweet and also strangely biting.

"I like ice cream, but I can't get it." Vi laid her spoon down in despair. "It flips away, just as I think I've got a spoonful."

"I don't like the goo," Henry said, "it's too sticky sweet. Let's put the ice cream in the saucer and eat it like a pudding. It can't get away then."

This we did, and though I felt a little guilty leaving the three tall foaming glasses of almost untouched soda, I found I already felt more kinship with tea and bread and butter than I did for these sickly sweet glasses of syrup.

"It was very nice," my guests told me dutifully. Nevertheless, as I signed the check, my cheeks burning at the pleasure of actually having and using a charge account all my own, I knew that from now on when I took people to tea, it would be real tea, the clear amber beverage itself with delicious butter crumpets or tea cake. Never again a sandwich and a soda. Somehow, here in London, sodas had lost their charm and seemed as out of place as a décolleté gown at breakfast-time.

When Vi and Henry left me off at Carleton Mansions, they were very agreeable. "Come see us soon," they insisted. "You've improved quite a lot. In fact, you're quite decent now. Good-by." And they were gone. I felt a great deal better. I'd seen something in their eyes and in their manners that hadn't been there before, something I'd never expected to see, either. I hurried upstairs to tell Mother all about my afternoon and what a nice time I'd had with Vi and Henry Mond.

chapter 7:   Mr. D'Auban the Elder

ALL THE excitement of being an American girl studying dancing in London had quieted down. Now I was just an ordinary
student going to class, eating, practicing, and going to see
dancing. To a large extent even the joy of watching great
dancers had disappeared, for I was beginning to see how they
accomplished their effects. I recognized steps; arm movements were no longer graceful flutters; the smiling lips, the
heaving bosoms, and the rigidly held knees were now part
and parcel of a dancer's conscious art. I even began to see
the individual difference in toe work: some dancers stabbed
the toe down like a dagger, as did Fanny Elssler. Others
drifted onto the toe rather like flower petals falling. Maria
Taglioni was supposed to have introduced this dreamy quality.

Dancers who stab and dancers who drift are in their ele-

ment when they are students. Never again will they revel in
their capacities to thrust or float as they can then. All about
me were girls in toe slippers who had decided on their métier.
I myself, recently on toe, had no difficulty in deciding which
approach was mine. The delicate butterfly approach was
the epitome of ballet, both in my mind's eye and in my
dreams.

In reality, I plodded about on toe with the delicate tread
of a baby elephant after a hearty meal.

"Hold the weight back and up. Do *not* clump!" Madame
raged at me. "Keep the knees straight. Move from the hips.
Do *not* wobble. Quickly now, the toe-tips like beads of light.
The *bourrées* must be like the sparks from the electric.
Queek, Queek!" Her hands flashed. I struggled and stumbled.
And then, one day, I fairly flew around the room. I passed
all the girls without thinking, though we were in line, going
round and round. For some completely unknown reason my
ankles were steady, my knees were straight, and the slight
undulation of my hips produced this strange skimming movement of my toes.

"A miracle. Stop all of you. Little wan. You see! You
do what I tell you, and you are danseuse. Again. You."
Madame never remembered my name. If I didn't answer to
you or to the pointer stabbed my way, she would shout,
"America, it is bad the way you hunch before the jump.
Shoulders back, mees. Head up. A little run, then, whooo."
She raised her arms to indicate that I would then take off
en l'air. This was my first praise from her, and to my surprise,
though I rose in favor with Madame, my stock fell to zero
with my classmates.

"Where've you been studying?"

"How'd you learn to dance like that?"

"Who d'you think she's kidding? She always did know 'ow.

She 'as been pulling our legs. No one learns to dance like that overnight."

"But honestly," I began, taking off my slippers. "I am just learning. I've been practicing and watching Anna Pavlova, and trying to do *bourrées* the way she does . . ." It was then that I realized that no one was listening. They were all in the room, but I was the little girl who wasn't there.

"They were perfectly horrid," I told my mother. "They acted so mean. You'd think they hated me. They weren't good sports at all."

"Of course not," Mother said quietly. "Stop and think, Regina. Here you are, a rank outsider, and an American into the bargain. As long as you're a bit odd, a bit funny, and not very good, you're a kind of joke these girls can take. But if suddenly something—that something which won you recognition by a producer like Mr. Stuart—shows through and is recognized, you are not one of the common herd, you're an outsider, a menace, a real threat to every single girl's one hope and desire, her chance to get a job. There are only a few solo parts for student dancers, as in every other field. Once real competition raises its ugly head, it's every girl for herself."

"But that's awful. I don't want to take jobs away from them. I just want to dance."

"I doubt that," Mother said gently. "You've simply never come face to face with supply and demand before. Sometime when there's only one job and you want it, you'll understand what I mean."

I shook my head and started to practice. That night at dinner I said suddenly, "I don't want to go back to Mr. D'Auban's. I hate the kind of dancing I do there. It's horrid. It's just nasty music hall, hip, hip, hop, hop, kick, kick, kick. He scolds all the time, too. He says I spoil the line, and he looks so crossly at me, I want to die." Here I promptly got hiccups, choked, wept, and was patted on the back.

Everyone at table talked at once. The German baron suggested I go for a ride instead of dancing the next morning. The Indian princes suggested we sight-see instead of my studying. A little culture would not come amiss. The Australians thought two teachers might be one too many for me, the Italian countess did not think anyone could study successfully with any teacher beside Zanfretta. Mother listened to everyone and said not a single word. She was watching my reactions.

Finally, an Englishman, a recent addition to our table, spoke up. He had just returned from an archaeological expedition in Egypt. A selection of the treasures he had dug up was laid out neatly on a table in the parlor. I had been admiring them before dinner, and he had been so gentle and so soft-spoken that I was surprised at his vehemence. "You must not stop, not until something happens! Some crisis." He spoke severely. "You must not leave anything unresolved! You will be sorry if you just give up. Wait and work. When the time comes for you to leave your Mr. D'Auban, a path will be opened and you will know what it is."

I sniffed, wiped my eyes, and ate my dinner. I practiced. We went to see Maude Allan dance. Her dancing seemed to lack the technique I considered essential. I did not then realize that the breaking away from balletic tradition was just beginning, and that Miss Allan was one of the first exponents of free, or modern, dance. Because I was bemused by ballet, an ardent balletomane and a ballerina, albeit a dramatic one, by choice and, perhaps, by preordination, any other kind of dancing left me quite unmoved.

At home my usual ten o'clock bedtime was ignored. After

I had practiced, we ate the sandwiches and milk laid out for us on our table. Mother didn't say a word. She just kissed me goodnight and went into the bedroom, which was hers. I slept on the couch in our sitting room.

"Do you want to be rubbed?" Mother opened the door to ask.

"No . . . thank you," I added belatedly from the window where I was watching the moon, a luminous pearly disc in a delicately grayish sky pricked with silver stars.

I went to bed undecided. It was a strangely lonely decision I had to make. Any mention of Mr. D'Auban had been scrupulously avoided since dinner. Whether I went to class or stayed home was entirely my own affair. What was more to the point, to my mind, was that I didn't like the kind of dancing I was doing with him, while I not only liked it at Zanfretta's, but was doing it well. One remark rankled. "Where did you learn to dance like that?" I did not know the answer. I felt fairly certain it was because for three months I had watched Pavlova move until her every motion was etched in my mind's eye, but could seeing be translated into action? Could . . . And then I was sure. I hated my lessons with Mr. D'Auban the Younger largely because I did them so badly and was a target for criticism, but I loved my lunches with Mr. D'Auban the Elder, his stories of Elssler and Taglioni. His tales of ballet, his reminiscences of how the great ballerinas had looked and what they had said. Even the mention of Queen Victoria, who loved ballet so devotedly as a child that she dressed many of her little wooden dolls as ballerinas, had intrigued me. How I would love to see those dolls. I made up my mind to look them up. Then and there my decision was made. I would go back to class with the Younger because I couldn't bear to leave the Elder.

At breakfast the next morning there was the most concerted, directed conversation ever. The weather got a good going-over. The newspaper was held up as a protection against questions. Comment on everything but me and my problem was crisp and incisive. I ate, having been spoken to but once with a courteous good morning. I went my way, polite nods speeding me. I went down the steps feeling a bit silly, but I went without a word. I had taken my mother's breakfast up. Seeing me dressed, she had smiled and said, "Thank you. Lovely day, isn't it?" I could have shaken her. Why didn't she ask what I was going to do? "I believe I'll go to the Tate Gallery," she added casually. "Have a good day, dear."

I arrived at Drury Lane. I changed. I danced. I could feel waves of disapproval when Mr. D'Auban the Younger looked at me. I did my very best, and all the girls looked at me askance.

"Waist-high kicks," Mr. D'Auban told the line. Invariably one of my legs flew too high, and he would click the nasty little mechanical snapper he had in his hand which told the line someone was out of step. Almost inevitably it was my fault, and it made the girls furious to have to stop and start over. Those who had their arms around my waist pinched hard while they smiled angelically and kicked at exactly the right height. Mother never could understand the black-and-blue marks around my waist.

"What an odd place for bruises," she would say when she rubbed me down with the fresh-smelling liniment Aunty Barb had made and sent us from home. "How do you ever manage to bump yourself there?" I didn't answer. Explanations were not only odious, but they would involve a long recital of woes which would certainly make Mother raise her eyebrows.

Once again, when the line separated and we began working in place, though we were supposed to be working in unison, old Mr. D'Auban appeared with his violin tucked under his chin. He often came from his office to walk about among us, playing along with the pianist with his own accented rhythm. He would also coach, cajole, comment, and praise some particular dancer. Today he stood longest beside me, and I danced my heart out for him.

"Father," Mr. D'Auban said, "you're encouraging her. She's bad enough without your helping her make a spectacle of herself. At this rate I'll never make a good line dancer out of her."

Class had halted. It was seldom the two men spoke together where we could hear. Suddenly I felt quite deflated and stupid. I hardly heard the Elder ask gently, "Why a line dancer, son? Why not a soloist?"

The Younger's laugh was cynical and shockingly rude. "Oh, come now, Father, you're kidding. She's impossible."

"Impossible in the line, but not as a feature dancer."

"Gad!" The Younger looked at him helplessly. "How can you say that? The kid doesn't know a *battement* from a *bourrée*."

This stirred me to comment. "I do, too." I said loudly. "*Battements* are kicks and these are *bourrées*." I did my newly acquired *bourrées* nonchalantly. They really were surprisingly fast, thanks to Zanfretta and Anna Pavlova.

Mr. D'Auban the Elder said, "See!" Mr. D'Auban the Younger shrugged his shoulders.

"Her *arabesque* is atrocious. She can't do a split or kick her head. She's headstrong, untrained, stubborn, and . . ." he hesitated, then added, "a damn nuisance in class."

"Then why not give her to me?" Mr. D'Auban suggested. "I'd like to train her."

"Take her, and welcome," the Younger said, and at the Elder's nod, I followed him out of class. Not averse to making the most of his exit, he fiddled furiously, and I skipped after him in a series of steps which amounted to nothing more than the caperings of a young goat half drunk with adulation.

In his big back-room studio I had often seen his only pupil, beautiful Lola Lee, not yet sixteen but already a successful music-hall performer. She moved with a lyric quality I panted to acquire. Hers, however, was natural-born grace wedded to skill by serious hard work. She tapped competently, she undulated as an Oriental dancer with uncanny ease, she flirted as a soubrette. Her high kicks were the highest I had ever seen. Front kicks rose like birds. Side kicks whacked her ears wickedly, back kicks had to be watched lest the toe of her slipper black her own eye when it was meant merely to tap her forehead. She rose and fell in the split with the ease of a serpent, and her back bends left me speechless. She bent over backward and then peered roguishly at you through her legs. And all this she did as casually as if it were child's play.

I watched Lola's lessons now, and sometimes, standing far in the back corner of the room, I was permitted to attempt the same adagio. As well ask a colt to follow a horse well trained in *haute école* to do *dressage*, but I tried. Especially I yearned for the fluid technique which made one motion flow into the next. At home I practiced with such vigor that I strained muscles, bruised myself from falls, and passed out from sheer exhaustion.

"I do believe you've gone quite mad," my mother said one day about two weeks later. "This cannot be good for you. I really think you quite lost consciousness the last time you fell. Surely you're not supposed to fall over backward learning to do back bends."

"No," I admitted, rubbing my head, "but I'm so dreadfully far behind Lola. She——"

"Lola!" Mother sat back and looked at me. "But Lola Lee is a professional dancer, a music-hall personality. She's been on the stage since she was six. You're not competing with her. She's a pupil of Mr. D'Auban the Elder. His only pupil."

"No, she's not," I whispered, my head going round and round in aching circles. "I'm his pupil too. He took me away from the Younger about two weeks ago."

"Really!" Mother looked amazed. "And why didn't you tell me?"

"I don't know," I whispered. "I was trying to prove something or other, but now I don't know what."

"Into bed with you," Mother said. "You've very likely got concussion of the brain or something. Lie flat, stop thinking, and sleep."

This I did. I slept all the next day and the next night. Mother fed me custard with a spoon. The third day I was up, feeling a little lightheaded.

"I telephoned Mr. D'Auban you had a slight cold," Mother explained. "How do you feel?"

"Floaty," I said. "I'd better practice, I guess."

"No more back bends," Mother said firmly, "unless you hold onto something. Use my bed. It's solid enough to hold your weight. Promise now?"

"I promise." I worked out, slowly at first, then faster. That afternoon the Baron drove me, an interesting invalid, in the park. He was most solicitous.

"Marry me, and you will never have to work like this again. I have a fine house and many retainers. You can have your own carriage."

"I prefer to dance," I told him, "though I do thank you for the honor."

At dinner that night Mother told the wondrous news that I was a pupil of D'Auban the Elder. Everyone was very pleased. The Baron bowed, and the Indian princes suggested a Sunday boat trip as a celebration. After dinner the Australians presented me with a small framed picture of Melbourne Harbour, a prized possession, but it was the English archaeologist who was most pleased.

"See," he said, "what I said was true. If you had given up and not gone back to class, you would have missed this golden opportunity. You must stay with a situation until it is resolved. If you do, success is within your grasp. Failure is almost invariably the result of quitting too soon. In digging, it is the last shovelful that counts, for it is the shovel that uncovers the treasure long after you and all about you have given up hope." He had led me to the table with his treasures, which he was preparing to pack up, since his business in London was finished.

"Choose something to remember this lesson by," he suggested. "Take anything you want."

I bent over the various tiny images, deities, and scarabs carved of a greenish turquoise-colored stone. I hesitated. What if I should pick the most valuable thing he had, something truly precious to him, whereas I would value it only as a talisman because he had given it to me.

"You choose," I begged. "I would rather have something you gave me."

He smiled, and his fingers unerringly chose a scarab. "This is a good luck scarab," he told me. "I will have it drilled and mounted in a ring for you. You will keep it always in remembrance of what I have told you. Success comes to the one who never quits."

I still have my green scarab. I look at it often. I have never had better advice than from this Englishman whose name I do not remember, but whose philosophy shaped my life.

chapter 8:   *Costumes and Competition*

ON THANKSGIVING DAY a most upsetting letter from Father told us that he had had a day in court and had been given extensions on various mortgages, as well as complete exoneration of any wrongdoing in having signed so many notes. "The judge said I was one of the most foolish, pigheaded men he'd ever met, first in signing, and then in being determined to pay all the notes in full, instead of going into bankruptcy; but he shook hands with me right there in the courtroom, and said he was proud to do so. Right now I am a little light-headed with all these goings-on."

I enjoyed the letters, but my mother lived, moved, and had her being in them. She carried them in her ample handbag and read them over and over. She was always writing Father a letter, or sealing one, or posting one. Father was so close in our thoughts that we seemed in constant communion.

All I could feel thankful for on this turkeyless Thanksgiving was the fact that I was in England and actually learning to dance. I was working more steadily now and less violently. Between them, Madame Zanfretta and Mr. D'Auban had convinced me that dancers are made over a period of time and growth, rather than out of frenzied performance.

Three months had changed me from an American schoolgirl to a hard-working student of the dance. Because of the special attention of my teachers and my own avid desire for knowledge, I soaked up everything about the subject until I was the bane of my companions' existence—teacher's pet. I didn't know or care. My teachers had something I wanted to learn, and I extracted information and made use of it with a completely one-track mind. I knew what I wanted and was perfectly happy.

Saturdays I had dance classes as usual, but I managed somehow to do a bit of shopping or take in a dramatic show. I saw and fell in love with Gerald du Maurier. Almost was I tempted to stop dancing and become a dramatic actress. Harry Lauder on Saturday nights also broke the spell of ballet, and I laughed and laughed and loved his every chuckle, the way he pounded the stage with his stick, the way he spraddled his legs and took us all into his confidence with his disarming smile and his gravelly voice.

Mother went out quite a lot. She met Sylvia Pankhurst and Lloyd George. I wasn't invited to big dinners. Though I was well along in my teens, I was rated a schoolgirl by my mother's friends, largely, perhaps, because I made no effort to grow up and dress like a young lady. Instead I was content with my blue serge skirts and white cotton blouses, my short jackets and berets. I had never used lipstick and I never did grow up to high heels. Because my idol, Anna Pavlova, wore a boy's blue chinchilla overcoat and low-heeled broad-toed childish oxfords to class, I considered clothes of little importance. No doubt Pavlova dressed exquisitely in the styles of the day, but I saw her only in costume on stage or going in and out of dance studios for practice sessions.

The ballet 1830 was being rehearsed at the Alhambra Theatre, next door to Madame Zanfretta's school. A number of us bribed the doorman with sweets, little tins of candied ginger, and Canton tea. Once inside, we hid in the boxes and stared down at the stage. However, we were sadly disappointed. It was a romantic musical-comedy type of ballet with Mr. Donald Clayton Calthrop in it rather than Nijinsky. There was Poldi Muller and Mr. Emile Agoust, Miss Greville Moore and a pair of American dancers called Adelaide and Hughes. The girls looked at me sadly. So that was American dancing! I disclaimed it violently, for I had no knowledge of musical-comedy acrobatic dancing and had no idea how good these two were from that standpoint. It just wasn't the kind of ballet dancing I loved; therefore I didn't like it.

"A pity we didn't bribe the Empire man and have a look at Kyasht," someone said. I agreed. The Alhambra show was a far cry from a rehearsal of *Sylvia*.

One Sunday Mother and I were taken to the Trocadero to dinner. It was quite the most magnificent restaurant I had ever been in. A side of roast beef as rare and delicious-looking as any Dickens ever wrote about was wheeled to us on a shiny silver cart. French pastries finished up the meal, leaving me gorged with food. I sat sipping my demitasse and reveling in the glorious fact that I really was learning to dance. I became aware of conversation relating to me when Mother turned and said, "You must ask Lola where she has her costumes made. Mrs. Mond has sent us five pounds. We are invited to Dr. Robert's home, Coombe-Bank in Seven Oaks, Kent, for a part of the Christmas holidays. She writes she expects you to dance and knows you will need pretty costumes."

"Oh, how simply stupendous!" I said, but even as I said it, I wondered what I would dance. The kind of costumes I bought would have to be for particular dances, and all I was doing was studying steps. I had nothing in shape to perform for a houseful of critical guests at a place like Coombe-Bank. I explained, or tried to, all the way home.

Mother shook her head in concern. "Then what are you doing if you're not learning dances?" she demanded. "Why the lessons?"

"I'm learning to dance," I said finally. "Kids who learn to swim don't swim the Channel the first months. Singers don't get leading roles in operas, artists don't get hung."

"And a great pity," Mother said briskly. "It would help art a lot if more painters were hung and fewer of their canvases."

"Mother, don't be so silly."

"What about those dances? Can't you learn some?"

"Yes," I said, and giggled. "I'll learn Lola's. I'll watch her lessons instead of practicing. They'll never guess, they'll just think I'm tired or something. I'll really pay attention to her steps and music, and watch where the cuts are and everything."

"Is that right?" Mother demanded. "Doesn't she pay Mr. D'Auban to make them up for her?"

"Yes, she does, but I can't do them the way she does. No one will ever know, and anyway, I'm not going to dance them in the theater, it's just kind of an amateur concert, isn't it?"

Mother nodded. "We go to Sir Jesse Boots's house at Bournemouth for Christmas week, then to Dr. Robert's for the week after. New Year's Day there and your birthday."

"How lovely. Now, my dances. Maybe I'd better ask Mr. D'Auban about them if I'm to have costumes."

93

Mother agreed, and I tackled him the next day. "Hmmm," he said. "Hmmm. I think we can work it out. A Hungarian military dance." He brought out a faded post card. "I did this one for years. Let your costumer make it up in white broadcloth with gold-braid, astrakhan cap and the cape lined with red satin. A soubrette. Choose your own color, but have the overskirt dark, the chiffon petticoat light. One ballet, I suppose. Just who are you studying ballet with? I'm getting curious."

"Why, how, how . . ." I stammered.

"How did I know?" he asked, his eyes twinkling. "Well, for one thing, you're getting very nicely turned out. You point your toes and you do steps I haven't taught you when I call out the names. Now how would you know how to do a glissade if you weren't studying elsewhere?"

I was looking down at the floor. "Madame Zanfretta," I mumbled.

"No wonder, but I wouldn't have thought she'd have taken you. You're a big girl to be starting ballet."

"She didn't really take me," I said, remembering that she had simply announced that I could try it for a week. "She said I could come on trial, and then she never did tell me I couldn't. Maybe she forgot."

Mr. D'Auban shook his head. "Madame is not one to forget," he told me. "She must have thought you had something to let you stay."

Soon I had my military dance down pat. Lola and her mother watched me and applauded. My soubrette work didn't please Lola, and to Mr. D'Auban's amusement she took over and taught me her dance herself. Soon we both were cavorting about, switching our skirts and shaking our rumps at a purely imaginary audience. Mr. D'Auban fiddled away, and we both had a wonderful time.

"Are you on toe?" Mr. D'Auban asked. I nodded. "Then

put your slippers on and I'll arrange you a pretty toe dance," he told me. "I know Madame won't. It'll be five years at least before she'd ever let you do a solo." I knew he was right, though I had not dared put the thought in words.

"Not bad," Mr. D'Auban said in surprise. "The Madame has indeed done wonders. You're nicely placed. Let me see. Jumps, pirouettes, *entrechats*. Just what do you know?"

I danced for him, but no longer was it a breathless performance of wild eccentricity. I had become pedantic and very careful. Each step was an entity, done as best I could do it.

"This is a surprise to me," he said slowly. "You are not really a music-hall entertainer at all. You are what we might call a good all-round dancer, and you may have the makings of a star performer. We'll go on that tack for a while. You have already passed Lola, that is why your dancing is making hers look a little shoddy. You'd better keep out of her private lessons from now on. If they don't know it already, they will very soon, and there'll be trouble."

"Trouble? I don't know what you mean." I stared at him in surprise. "What kind of trouble?"

"The usual," he said, sighing. "When a person passes another in a competitive field, there's no love lost. If you don't know that yet, you've some hard lessons coming to you."

I lifted my shoulders. I didn't believe a word of what he was saying, not until a few days later, when Lola's mother shut the studio door in my face, saying, "Lola paid for a private lesson, and I don't want her distracted. She has been spending a great deal of her time teaching you, and we can't afford it. She is booked for a long tour of the provinces and must get up her repertoire."

The door shut, then opened again. Mr. D'Auban peeped out. "Go practice with my son, or go into my office and read."

I went into the office. I looked at pictures of great ballerinas—Carlotta Grisi, Fanny Elssler, Maria Taglioni, Chessinskaya, Zambelli, Pavlova—and I thought and wondered about them all. So many stories, such strange rumors. Even Pavlova and Mordkin had had a fight. One night Pavlova ran and leaped into the air and fell because Mordkin was not there to catch her. She slapped him, and he slapped back. Such a scene. No one ever knew who was right. Pavlova insisted he should have been one place; he, another. Was it temper, an honest mistake, or an intentional blunder?

For the first time I realized that dancers were people, with human frailties. They weren't just technically proficient automatons in fragile filmy frocks, with graceful arms, silken legs and immaculate toe shoes. The set smile, the flashing teeth, and the shining braided hair were all part and parcel of the pageantry, but the dancer within her cocoon of tarlatan and tinsel was a person who loved and hated, suffered and enjoyed, fought and took what she desired most from life.

My friendship with Lola was at an end. Without a discourteous word ever having been spoken, we now merely bowed and stood back politely and passed the time of day. No longer was I the amusing little American; I was rather that girl from the States who had no sense of thine or mine and was horning in on people's private lessons, and all because, somehow or other, my dancing had become good enough to be a challenge instead of a joke.

The principal dancers of a number of different companies often took class together at Madame Zanfretta's at twelve o'clock. Now that Lola had gone away and I had been promoted at Zanfretta's from beginners to an intermediate class, I went in the morning, arriving at eight-thirty. We were all supposed to be out of the dressing rooms and the studio before the stars arrived, but I contrived to dawdle around, darning someone's slippers or tights, filling the watering can, wiping the *barre*, even emptying a wastebasket so that I could catch a glimpse of these great dancers chatting together and casually trying to outdo each other in *battements* and *arabesques*.

Pavlova came in one day in a little raggedy tutu and hand-knitted gray shawl, a pair of slippers in her hands. Seeing me, she stopped, smiled, and beckoned.

"*La petite Americaine.* What are you doing here? You are a student?"

I nodded.

"Show me. A *battement.* A glissade. An *arabesque.*"

My toe shoes were very old and worn, but I did the best I could. Madame looked at me sharply.

"Good shoulders. Good knees. Good head. But the back!" She pounded with her fist on my bare back. "In here! In at the waist. Up so!"

"Slippers?" she asked, handing me hers. "Try them. I was going to put them in the chest."

I nodded dumbly. The chest, that thing that looked like a woodbox, proved to be full of slippers. How could it be that I had never known they were there for all to use freely? I must have seen dancers go to it and come from it many times, but it had never occurred to me what it was.

"Yours?" I asked, and she nodded, smiling.

"In the beginning the height is of no importance," she explained. "First the back must be right for the *arabesque*. Always the leg must be turned out. Then, only then, the height will come of its own accord." She moved away, spoke suddenly over her shoulder. "Show me again when you improve. Work now. Work always!"

"I will," I promised. "I really will."

"She spoke to you."

97

"She gave you her slippers."

"Let me touch you for luck." I thought the girl was fooling, and I turned, smiling, but her face was blankly serious, her eyes fierce with intense smoldering fire. Her touch troubled me, as the others, half amused, but no less anxious for good luck, reached out to touch me, too. The room was quiet now as we dressed.

"Pavlova never spoke to *me*," someone said aloud. "Some people 'as all the luck. Money for private lessons and 'igh and mighty friends."

"I'm getting my lessons practically free," I said, "and my friends aren't the kind who will get me a job."

"Tiking the bread right out of a poor girl's mouth, I sye," one girl spoke loudly. "Wot's Miss Ameriky doing with practically free lessons?"

"If they weren't practically free," I said boldly, "I wouldn't be here. I'd be back in the U.S.A."

"And a pity it is you ain't, what with all your sucking up to the balleyrinas, the wie you do. I'd be ashimed, I would."

"I do *not* suck up. I admire Madame Pavlova——"

"Out!" Madame Zanfretta looked like a thundercloud. "Such noises. Get out of here, and not a word. Do you understand? Not one single word!"

We stood frozen. Madame's accent was gone completely. She spoke as good English as we did. And then I realized that her broken English, her mixture of languages, was gentle, friendly camouflage, for she had dancers of every nation working with her, and to have spoken every language fluently and well would have seemed to give her a superiority she did not need. Her knowledge of ballet was what they came for, and she gave it to them with graciousness, with open hands and open heart to make them better dancers and thus raise the standards of dance a little higher than before.

98

The year 1911 is often spoken of as a time when ballet was at a very low ebb in England. Maybe it was, but I thought it was high. Karsavina, Nijinsky, Pavlova, Mordkin, Genée, Kyasht, Lopokova, Phyllis Bedells . . . To me it was a star-studded world of brilliant ballerinas and *danseurs nobles* whom I shall always cherish and revere.

chapter 9:   *The Gold Piano*

I WAS BUSIER than ever, but despite all my activity, I never lost the strange sensation that I was being watched critically instead of being babied and admired. I had no way of knowing that this was a part of growing up in any art. While one is clumsy and cute, it is easy to excite amused, half-contemptuous applause, but when one begins to be good enough to provide competition, indulgence flies out of the window.

My first costumes proved dreams of delight. I saw nothing whatever wrong with them. I particularly loved my military uniform, and marched about in it with such whippings and turnings and snappy salutes that Mother became bored.

"You might as well have gone to West Point," she told me, "if that's all you've learned at dancing school."

"I don't go to dancing school," I explained. "Ballet class is quite different from dancing school."

"It must be." Mother pursed her lips. "All you do is halt and about face."

"Wait till you see me in the other costumes," I begged. "Maybe you really ought to come to class."

"Quite the contrary." Mother buttoned the cuffs of her white embroidered shirtwaist. "I don't want to see any of your dances till you dance at the Monds'. I want to see you as others see you. I will then, perhaps, have some idea of how you dance."

I accepted her verdict with as good grace as I could, though I couldn't refrain from crowing when I came home the next day.

"I am to appear at a soiree given by a French countess who lives here in London," I explained. "She came to see Mr. D'Auban and wanted Lola, but she took me because Lola is away on tour."

"Do you get paid?" Mother asked practically.

I shook my head. "She will send her carriage for me, give me a little present, and send me safely home again."

"Hmmm," Mother said. "When is this?"

"The nineteenth of December."

"I am dining with the Monds. I will meet Lloyd George again. I find him an odd man. I do *not* think I am a Liberal. I feel Sir Alfred goes too far."

"You mean his going to India?"

"I do not," Mother said. "Policy, plans for the future."

"The future is far away," I said.

"Don't argue about things you know nothing about," Mother said crossly. "You'll be as bad as those silly women throwing bricks through beautiful plate-glass windows. I am a suffragette, but I do *not* think beautiful windows should be broken, nor that delicate females should go to jail for the vote. It's uncivilized. Women should get what they want through tact and charm."

"But you get cross and wave your umbrella when you can't get what you want by being nice."

"That is quite different," Mother answered. "When people are stupid, one has to shout and push!"

"Maybe that's the way the suffragettes feel."

"No doubt," Mother agreed, "but I only wave my umbrella, I don't break things with it."

"I have to go see this Countess Sans Nom at lunchtime tomorrow," I said. "Can you imagine me visiting a countess?"

"No, I can't," Mother said flatly. "Do you suppose she's a real countess or just a fake?"

"I don't know," I admitted, "and I don't suppose I ever will. How could I tell?"

"Not by looking at her," Mother answered with a slight smile, "but we can look her up in *Burke's Peerage*. That will settle it. I'll do that next time I go out."

The Countess proved quite real when looked up, and I went to call on her in fear and trembling. All told, it was queerer than if she had been bogus. I took a hansom, and the horse was a good strong horse and trotted briskly to the address. I was expected, ushered into a small jewel-box of an *ascenseur*, and wafted high in the interior of a large town house. A maid in black taffeta with a frilly apron conducted me down a hall carpeted in opalescent-hued white to a room whose great bay window opened on tree tops and sky. The rugs were white, the walls, pink, the furniture, gold. It was as unbelievable as a Christmas Pantomime, and continued so.

The Countess was in a great gold bed with pale pink sheets and a rosebud puff. Her hair was much more glittery than the gold plate from which she was eating. A rich, dark liquid was in a soup plate, and delicate golden brown *croissants* with butter petals were on a tray before her. She ordered chocolate and rolls for me. They must have been waiting, for they appeared as if by magic. The chocolate was too thick to drink, so I, too, spooned it up. She talked pleasantly, but treated me as negligently as if she were planning to hire me as a scullery maid.

"You will come at eleven, to the tradesmen's door. You will be in costume. No changing, you understand. You will wait in the butler's pantry. A footman will bring you in. The orchestra will have your music. You will do two numbers, in the same costume."

"Would you like soubrette or ballet?" I asked. "I have a golden-brown soubrette dress with red cherries and pink under petticoats and a white ballet frock with pink roses."

"The brown thing. God forbid a classic ballerina in my drawing room. It might distract the gentlemen."

I wondered from what, but I forbore to ask. "The music?" she asked.

I gave the names, shuffling the music as I did so to show the titles. "It's cut properly," I explained, "but if they play too fast, I'll have trouble. . . ."

"It makes no difference." She motioned her tray away. "Just drift around and look pretty. Go and play some of this stuff and I'll tell you which ones to dance."

"Play?"

"On the piano, of course."

I turned, and there behind me was a gold piano decorated with the most exquisitely painted miniature cherubs. A gold piano! I hardly dared touch its delicately beautiful ivory keys. A gold piano in one's bedroom! Chocolate in a gold soup plate eaten with a spoon, and an artist using the kitchen entrance like a charwoman. All as odd and confused as if I were dreaming it all. In fact, Mother was hard put to accept my account of my morning's visit.

"Really, Regina, you must be out of your mind. Do you think it is funny to come home with such a story? Surely you don't expect me to believe this nonsense about gold pianos with cherubs painted on and hot chocolate in a gold soup plate!"

"But it's true. Honestly, Mother, it's true. She looks kind of enameled herself, all pink and white, and her hair is so shiny, it doesn't look real."

"No doubt a wig." Mother raised her eyebrows. "Well, we'll just have to put it down to experience."

It was an experience, no doubt of that. I drove off in a purple carriage with gray horses and two men in plum-colored livery. The carriage smelled deliciously of violets. There wasn't a trace of stable odor. I sat stiffly, my skirts around me, well away from the back of the seat. I had on my first rouge, powder, and lipstick. I went over my steps in my mind. The kitchen was a beehive of industry, and I picked my way among white-clad cooks and liveried waiters, balancing trays of empty glasses on high. Hors d'oeuvres, pastries, great brown fowls, were laid out on huge platters. In the pantry I stood nervously as panting, perspiring men rushed by me, to pause, take a deep breath, push open the swinging door and march out with solemn tread and composed blank faces.

"You, Miss. Come now." A footman beckoned, the door opened for me, I heard strains of my music. I hurried out into two great rooms, full of people on little gold chairs, fanning themselves, chattering and drinking. The men, in evening clothes, their white shirt fronts crumpled, bent solicitously close to the most extreme décolletages I had ever seen. Diamonds glittered and pearls glistened; the air was heady with perfume.

It was very hot. Flowers scented the night and vied with the synthetic odors of musk and ambergris. A protecting wall of palms and ferns obscured the platform on which a stringed orchestra was playing. The first violinist cut the music short, caught my eye, and started over. A feeble spatter of applause sounded from the front rows as I appeared. There was no room at all to dance! I was in my audience's lap. I could only move gracefully, hither and yon, and do a few *arabesques* and poses. Any attempt to dance would result in chaos. Ferns would fall, vases break, ladies' laps would be full of me, a seemingly frenzied puppet. I moved in what I hoped would be taken for dance, but despite my utmost care, narrowly escaped tripping up a hurrying waiter with full complement of champagne on his uplifted tray, he having decided to lift it aloft at the very moment that I essayed a high side kick. By dint of great dexterity he escaped, and I, for safety's sake, settled into a low back bend.

My next dance was much gayer, and I proceeded to make a great to-do with my feet, quick darting little steps and a number of brisk turns and flutterings with the arms. It was the sort of behavior a frightened bird at a window might have indulged in, but it took the audience's fancy, and I was quite heartily applauded. I bowed, was given an armful of carnations, a large box, and a small envelope.

On the way out of the kitchen, one of the cooks handed me another box. "Yer a pretty thing," she told me. " 'Ere's a box of kikes."

"Thank you," I said. "Oh, look, let me dance a thank-you for it." And in the suddenly cleared space, I whirled and twirled through the dances I had not been able to do in the drawing room. The applause was loud, and I fear service stopped completely. I felt as Mischa Ellman must have when he was told by a hostess who had hired him to play that he was not invited to dinner and would please use the kitchen entrance. He had replied, "In that case, Madame, the fee will be much less."

Into the carriage, breathless and happy, I tumbled, clutching my music, given me punctiliously by the footman after

I'd danced, my boxes beside me. I peered into the envelope. There was no money inside, just tickets to a concert and a card of thanks. Back at the pension I was greeted with acclaim, equaled only by the acclaim the box of cakes received. Three were set aside for me, the others promptly eaten with exclamations of delight.

First, first I must open my gift and then I must dance again, that is if I was not too tired. "I am never too tired to dance," I said extravagantly, "but I do want to open my parcel." When I did, I could hardly believe my eyes. The loveliest French lady doll imaginable, with jointed kid body, exquisitely modeled face, and long brown hair. She had a complete trousseau, with the name *Lady Betty* embroidered on it. "I'm too old, really, for dolls," I admitted, "but I just love her." The other guests did too, and all of us spent more than one evening at the pension in dressing and undressing Lady Betty.

And then I danced. The furniture was moved back. A gentle little woman who had slipped in and out inconspicuously for weeks took her place at the piano.

"Let me have your music, dear," she said, and played it over and over again till we got it exactly right.

This, the third time I danced, everything was just as it should be. I had ample space. My music was played precisely as it should be played. I was dancing to an audience of friends and artists. I did my steps as Mr. D'Auban intended I should do them. This time the performance was a real success. I was applauded sincerely, complimented, and patted on the back. I ate my cakes and drank my tea in an atmosphere of love and understanding.

Mother arrived and joined in the fun. It took days to get the earlier events of the evening cleared up. "You danced in the Countess' drawing room. You danced in her kitchen. Then you came home and danced here! How come you didn't dance on the sidewalk?" Mother demanded, but little did she know that one day soon that was just exactly what I hoped to do. The troupes of street musicians, players, and dancers fascinated me, and someday I intended to go along with one of them.

"What an exquisite gift," Mother said of the doll. "Regina, I believe I will make her some clothes. Some crepe de Chine underthings, all hand-embroidered. You must keep her always. Perhaps sometime you will have a little girl of your own, and Lady Betty will be an heirloom doll."

chapter 10:   *Sidewalk Dancers*

CHRISTMAS was approaching. Mr. D'Auban was anxious for me to be in a pantomime.

"He says I need the experience of dancing in public," I explained. "Just in the chorus or a very small part. Couldn't I? I'd love it."

"Positively not." Mother shook her head firmly. "You seem to forget we have been invited by the Bootses for the Christmas holidays and on to Sir Robert Mond's for the New Year. Not only have we accepted, but you have promised to dance for Mrs. Mond, and you have accepted money with which to pay for your costumes."

"But Mrs. Mond's is just a private affair," I answered. "Isn't a real job at maybe three pounds a week more important? Wouldn't Mrs. Mond understand that I have to get on with my career?"

"Mrs. Mond would understand that you don't keep your word and that you take money under false pretenses. Chances are you'd go backward instead of forward in your career." Mother spoke tartly. "Keep your word. When you say you'll do a thing, do it. There's no substitute for dependability."

When I explained to Mr. D'Auban that I'd promised to dance at Mrs. Mond's and that she had paid for my costumes, he agreed with Mother that if I had said I'd dance, then dance I must.

"Let's see what you've done to your dances," he suggested. "Ten to one there's little left of the steps I taught you. Are you using the same music?"

I blushed very red. "In one dance," I admitted.

"Let's see the drill!"

I did it as I had revised it. He stopped me halfway through, bowed furiously on his violin, shook his head, and shouted, "No good. Do it the way I taught you, or have you forgotten?"

After a few false starts I had to admit I had. He retaught me, and in spidery hieroglyphics wrote the steps down.

"Now practice those," he said briskly. "Your revision has no military value at all. Dances must be true to type, and you've made it a wishy-washy mixture of music hall and ballet. Now what have you done to the *Soubrette?*"

Again the bow rapped sharply. "No go. No zip. Nothing's any good but the tilt of the head and the come-hither eyes. Where'd you get that, I'd like to know! It can't be taught. You must be growing up." Feeling very much let down, I learned the sequence of steps over again. For three days we worked on the two dances.

"Let me see them in costume tomorrow," Mr. D'Auban told me. "Now for the toe dance. Lord only knows what you've done to it, but let me have a look."

I hated to let him see it. It was entirely new. I had rebelled at the balletic clichés he had given me as a routine and had finally chosen new music and titled my dance, *Ballet Examination*.

"It's a story dance," I said. "I start it by putting my shoes on before the audience."

"Putting your shoes on! And why before the audience?"

"It's pantomime. I show how scared I am of the examination and how my feet hurt. And then I stand around and wait, and then I dance, and I think I've failed, for everyone else gets their certificates and I don't. . . ."

"And then I suppose you win the star role and head the ballet company?" he asked.

"I do *not!*" I cried. "My certificate just got stuck to another girl's, and she gives it to me, and I stop crying."

"Hmmm. Not bad at all," Mr. D'Auban said. "But the question is, what does it look like when you dance it? Could anybody understand?"

"I don't know," I admitted. "I haven't dared ask anyone if they could."

"You have to dance it shortly. You'd better show it to me, and we'll see what I can make of it." He propped my music up on the stand he so seldom used. I pulled a low stool center stage and sat on it.

"Will you have curtains at the Monds'?"

"I've no idea!" I faced the question for the first time with some shock.

"Better plan your entrance then," he told me. "It's easy to cut out, but you shouldn't leave an entrance to chance."

"What'll I do?" I asked helplessly.

"How should I know? You say you composed the dance, now just go ahead and compose the entrance."

"I'll come on pretending to tie the last layer of my tutu," I said, "like this. I'll be in stocking feet with my slippers round my neck, hanging by the ribbons. The pretend-mirror is here. Then I'll sit down and put my slippers on before it and do my dance."

"Very good." Mr. D'Auban approved until I tried it. "No. No!" The bow rapped sharply. "You're too sure of yourself. Wander in, be startled at sight of yourself in the mirror. Fix your headdress, then sit down."

I did it over three or four times, then told him. "I'm sorry, Mr. D'Auban, but I *am* sure of myself in the beginning, it's when I get my shoes on and start dancing for the examining board that I get panicky. It's no good if I get panicky twice."

He played a sort of chattery sound on his violin as if he were disagreeing with me, but said only, "It's your dance. Do it your way."

This time he didn't stop me, and I sped on stage, preened myself before the mirror, pulled on my satin shoes, adjusted the ribbons, and strutted about on toe until I got the feel of them. As soon as I could move easily and comfortably, I took my place in line. Now I fidgeted, and watched the first two dancers anxiously as they took their examination. Then I proceeded to do the steps called out by my imaginary examiners. Once or twice Mr. D'Auban chuckled. Then as I watched each girl given her certificate while I remained empty-handed, I drooped, my face crumpled, my chin sank to my chest. I was quite crushed until a paper thrust into my hand by a girl beside me proved to be the missing certificate. I smiled, brushed the tears away, pirouetted happily, and bowed low.

"Not half bad," Mr. D'Auban said. "For an amateur effort it is really quite good. It's a little ornate and you're inclined to be repetitive. You're long on the diagonal and short on circular movement. You cover the stage pretty well, but it is altogether too simple and too much the same. Those glissades of yours would be far better done in a half-circle, your *arabesques* would be quite interesting if done in five different positions in five different places on stage. As for your *bourrées*, they're quite the best thing you do. Why not link your steps with eight or ten of them and thus get your breath?"

"Gracious," I was breathless now for sure. "You mean it's all right? That I can do it?"

"It's not right at all yet," Mr. D'Auban answered. "But we can make it so. We'll stay with it today. Tomorrow we'll really set it. Now let's get on with the glissades. Half-circle, full stage. Left to right."

We worked till I finally sat down on the floor in exhaustion, my knees folding under me like a rag doll's.

"Go wash up," Mr. D'Auban told me. "I'll make some tea. Got your food with you?"

I nodded, and went off to the dressing room. I felt at ease for the first time in several weeks. My original dances had been pulled into shape, and now that I was being drilled on them and had had the benefit of criticism and advice, though I felt less excited and elated, I felt much happier and more confident.

"How long have you been making up your own dances?" Mr. D'Auban asked me. He had taken away my meat sandwich and substituted for it three thin slices of bread and butter and a wedge of cheese. My tea was hot and sugared. His regulation of my lunches must have taught me one of a dancer's cardinal rules of health, and that was, simple light nourishing food in small quantities, except after a performance and before a night's rest.

"Always," I answered. "When I was a very little girl, only about five years old, my mother gave me a blue ballet frock trimmed with pink paper roses for a Christmas present. I must have gone to some children's dancing school recital, because I was wild to dance myself. I pranced and twirled round our music room wearing scarves and flowers, and my mother had no peace because I wanted a blue ballet dress. Finally she told me that on Christmas I would have a surprise present. 'It's big enough to go all around the house and small enough to come inside it,' she told me. I puzzled over what it could be, and for days I helped my Aunty Barb make pink tissue-paper roses, winding the wire stems with green paper, thinking they were for table decorations. Christmas came. I received several dolls, a cradle, jewelry, candy, and a new coat, but the only thing I really cared about was the blue tarlatan ballet dress trimmed with *my* pink paper roses. There was a wreath of pink roses for my hair, and pink slippers to go with the pink silk stockings. I wore the dress all day long, and I danced and danced and danced.

"Mother let me have some lessons when I was six, but I wasn't a regular pupil anywhere," I went on. "We lived way out in the country on top of a hill. As I grew up, I rode horseback and played with the dogs. I had a governess, and for a few months each fall I would go to a school. Then the snow would come, the roads would be glare ice, and I'd be reduced to reading, playing the piano, sewing, and cooking. Not that I cared. I would rather stay home and dance and read and listen to stories than go to school. At twelve I was sent off to boarding school. Father had lost a lot of money on a note he'd signed for a friend, Mother had to go to the hospital for an operation. School was nice, but lessons were hard and I was unused to rules or discipline. The only thing I really loved was gymnasium and our dance lessons in the Dalcroze system. Somehow I cut all the outdoor sports and all our gym classes, but I managed to be in every one of the Dalcroze lessons, whether they were for first-, second-, or third-year students. I guess I was in class every day from one-thirty till five-thirty. We didn't really seem to have any steps like ballet, but we did count and move to music."

"How long?" Mr. D'Auban asked, and I answered, "Three years."

"That would explain it." He nodded. "It never made sense your learning to dance so quickly, but if you've had a childhood of fancy dancing along with three full years of daily Dalcroze instruction, the whole thing hangs together. You seem to know how to do something almost as soon as you're shown, for you've the basic ability, though it is latent because you've never had any formal training in any kind of dance."

"I don't understand," I said helplessly.

"I was just thinking aloud," he explained. "There's no need for you to understand. Bring your costume tomorrow," he added. "Put your hair up in braids around your head. You dance too well to leave it flopping about like a tapper."

I braided my hair when I got home, but I pinned it up around my ears rather than around my head. I felt silly with it up, my ears stuck out, and those beautiful shiny coronet braids looked like the ones worn by ballerinas from the Imperial Russian Ballet School, La Scala, or the Paris Opera. I would pin the braids around, then yank the pins out.

"Whatever is the matter with you?" Mother asked. "It looks very nice that way. Dinner is ready. Come on down as you are. The gong has rung."

"No!" I again coiled the braids into buns around my ears. "I like them better this way. Up on my head I feel as if people would raise their eyebrows and wonder if I thought I was another Karsavina. I know I'm not. I just can't wear my braids round my head."

"Then don't!" Mother was calmly impersonal. "No one cares how you wear it, up, down, or sideways. It's the way you dance that counts, not the way you wear your hair."

Every weekend we continued to sight-see. We saw the Crown Jewels, having paid our sixpence at the Tower. We

114

walked for miles around London, for Mother adored the historical significance of everything she saw. She loved the names of famous personages, and methodically checked off the places and people in her *Baedeker* with a little gold pencil. Then we would stand pressed against the railing outside the iron cage which housed the Crown Jewels for what seemed to me to be hours. I tired of the glittering baubles, but she never did.

"*St. Edward's Crown*," Mother pointed. "Stolen in 1671 by Colonel Blood, but he didn't escape with it. And the *King's Crown* made in 1838 for Queen Victoria. It has 2818 diamonds, three hundred pearls and the uncut ruby (spinel) in the front was given to the Black Prince in 1367 by Don Pedro of Castille . . ."

"Mother," I'd complain, "I can read it in the case and in *Baedeker*, do you *have* to tell it to me in such a loud voice? Everyone is listening."

"If everyone else is listening, you might learn a bit by listening yourself," Mother said shortly. "You're that edgy, I've an idea you're practicing a dance in your head, and my lecture is falling on deaf ears."

"It is," I said. "Mother, I must go back and practice. I have only one more lesson with Mr. D'Auban. I'm getting scared. Mrs. Mond is used to seeing very good dancing. She may think mine is just awful."

"I wouldn't worry." Mother led the way to the bus. "You're an invited guest, she and her friends will surely be polite."

That evening Mother went off to a dinner party. I danced. I tried on my costumes. After supper with some of the other guests I sat outside on the stone steps in a gypsy costume I'd made from some gaily colored scarves, worn over a full petticoat with a white embroidered blouse. I liked practicing in costume, but Mother had warned me not to wear my soubrette or ballet costume to practice in lest I spoil their freshness. As several of us chatted in the unexpectedly warm winter night, a band of street singers and dancers stopped before us. The women wore full black skirts and big hats, a girl was dressed as a tramp, the men were in worn evening clothes with tall hats. They danced a bit and sang. An elderly man walked with them, playing on a small violin. Seeing me in gypsy dress, he struck up a tune and said, "Come on now, Missy, and give us a breather. Dance for your friends a bit."

As I was dying to do this very thing, I was dancing before he got the words out of his mouth. At the end of my dance, the girl in the tramp suit passed the hat. As they walked on, I chatted with the violinist. If a man was over fifty and wore a beard, as my father did, I felt sure he was the soul of honor and everything a gentleman should be. I danced three more times, feeling entirely at home with the troupe and not noticing or caring how many corners I turned. It was growing dark, and the street lights were on. People had left their stoops. The fact that it was really winter was suddenly borne in on us when drops of cold, clammy rain began to fall.

" 'Ere now," one of the men in the troupe said rudely. "You'd best leg it home. You're a case you are, horning in like that."

"I was asked," I answered hotly. "*He* asked me."

"Ho! Pops! He's got an eye for a gel, still." The man snorted. "Know your way home?"

"No." I looked around nervously. It was quite dark. I was cold, wet, and suddenly a little frightened of these strange, rather unfriendly people. When they danced and laughed and joked for audiences, they had seemed so gay and kind; now they just seemed tired and suspicious and anxious to be rid of me.

"I'll take her back," the tramp girl said. "Then I'll take

the tube home. You go on. Be seeing you." She waved them off and took my arm. "It's not so far," she told me. "We went all around the block, before moving on. I thought if I sent you back with one of the men, he might get in trouble. Like as not someone'll be thinking we'd kidnaped you."

"Oh, no." I laughed in relief. "Don't worry. My mother always says if anyone ever did kidnap me, they'd bring me back fast. I'm too hard to handle."

"Good for you." The girl looked at me and laughed. "Same here. It's my troupe. We do piers and things summertimes. We go into the provinces after Christmas. I'm going to be a good actress someday."

"And I'm going to be a good dancer," I answered her.

We shook hands on it as we said simultaneously, "Wish you luck."

"There's your house." She pointed. "Are you all right now?"

"Sure," I agreed. "Thanks a lot." I started off.

"Hey, wait." She caught my sleeve. "We made more with you than we ever did alone. I'd take you on if we were regulars." She shoved a piece of silver into my hand. "That's for you."

"I don't want to take any money. . . ." I argued.

"You earned it," she said earnestly. "That fat man smoking a big cigar gave me this florin for you. He said you weren't half bad." She closed my fingers around the coin.

"My goodness," I said, looking at her in surprise. "My goodness me!" How ironic to have danced at a countess's soiree and been given a doll, and then to dance on the streets and earn real money.

" 'By now." She smiled and tugged at her cap, then hurried off. I realized as I looked after her that she was a grown woman, not a girl.

Back inside the pension I was scolded a little for my adventure into the unknown, stationed before the fire, and plied with hot tea. My florin was eyed respectfully.

"My first money," I said softly. "I am going to buy something for my father with it." I shopped carefully the next day and sent off a handsome leather-covered address book, suitably inscribed to "My dear, darling papa."

chapter 11:   *Christmas Vacation at Coombe-Bank*

In no time at all we were packed and had said good-by to
everyone at Carlton Mansions. A great many people were
going away for the holidays. There were also a great many
people coming. At the request of the proprietor we agreed
to sublet our rooms. The arrangement was very nice for us
because we had to count our pennies carefully.

Christmas at the Bootses' was a friendly affair. I was
treated like a young lady. Rita had many friends, and we
were invited out almost every day for lunch or tea. Evenings
we played games or charades with the grownups. The most
exciting event of the holiday was the night we were permitted to attend a Christmas ball being given at a neighbor's
home.

To my horror, I found I was an appalling ballroom dancer.
I was afraid of having my own feet stepped on, so I stepped

on my partner's. I also pushed and pulled him about to avoid collisions with other couples, which he would certainly have avoided, except for my interference. Rita danced exquisitely and was much sought after by many young men. I danced abominably and was not sought out by anyone but a young footman who gave me a note. It was from my mother, and suggested that as I appeared to think social dancing was some sort of wrestling match, it might be wise for me to refrain from attempting it and settle for being a professional entertainer.

Fortunately for my hurt feelings, Rita arrived to say we could go in to supper, but that we must then go home, as it was after midnight. This met with my approval. She was nice enough about it, but I knew she would have loved to stay.

After Christmas the Bootses arranged lovely coaching trips for us. Rita and I especially enjoyed sitting on the box beside the coachman, seeing the clever way he handled the four mettlesome horses and hearing the golden notes of the horn blown from the rear of the coach. I suppose if my head had not been filled with dreams of a stage success, I'd know a great deal more about the country I saw, but it is now merely an ecstatic blur of towns and meadows, frozen gardens, watery sunshine, and chill winds. We stopped for lunch and tea at various inns and warmed ourselves before the fire. While we ate, the horses were changed, and soon we were speeding off, chattering and laughing on our sight-seeing jaunts.

We saw Stonehenge and ruined cathedrals; we climbed broken stairways and admired lovely views; but always I was glad to get home to practice and have a hot bath. The evenings I showed improvement were red-letter evenings, for only then did I feel like myself.

At last came New Year's Day. The last family party was over. I said good-by to Rita, and we climbed into the Rolls Royce that was to take us to Sir Robert's home, Coombe-Bank in Seven Oaks, Kent. It was a lovely drive, but after our coaching experiences, sitting still in a glassed-in car seemed very dull. If anyone thinks that one sits still coaching, he is very much mistaken. One rides the coach fully as actively as one would ride a horse, and what with the bouncing, the slipping and sliding and the sudden stops, there were times when it was a most exhausting business.

At Coombe-Bank we were welcomed by Mrs. Ludwig Mond and her son, Dr. Robert Mond, the archaeologist, and his two daughters. They were little girls, not more than seven or eight, as I remember. Sir Alfred, Lady Violet, and their children, Henry and Violet, were also expected. Mother was drawn into conversation, tea was brought in, and then, to my surprised consternation, I was carried off by an English nanny to have tea with Dr. Robert's children in the nursery. After that indignity, I was taken to see their playhouse. As this was an adorable one-story cottage with thatched roof, quite large enough for a real family to live in, I was soon happy enough playing house with the two little girls.

Vi and Henry arrived, and we all had supper in the nursery. At eight the two youngest went off to bed. Vi and Henry, though younger than I, were certainly too old to be packed off to bed so arbitrarily. Nanny left us, suggesting books, cards, games and charades to keep us occupied.

"I have to dance," I said, remembering the big party on January fourth, my birthday, even though this party for the grownups had nothing whatever to do with it. "I think I ought to practice," I said virtuously.

"Why don't we go down to the ballroom and look it over," Henry suggested. "The stage isn't finished, but it is all built

121

and the curtains are hung. I saw them as I came by. You can see how much room you'll have to dance in. That'll help you a lot, and it'll be something to do."

Such a good idea! We hurried through halls and corridors, turning this way and that, and finally arrived at the huge mirror-lined ballroom in which I was to perform. Once Henry switched on the lights, I was struck dumb. Painted white and gold with glittering crystal chandeliers and little gold rose-brocaded chairs, the ballroom was the most magnificent I had ever seen. The floor was highly waxed and very slippery, but fortunately for me a stage had been constructed at one end which was quite adequate for a single dancer.

"I'll get into practice clothes if you'll wait here," I told Vi and Henry, and hurried off. But it was fully fifteen minutes later that I returned, convoyed by an amused footman, for I had not been able to find our own rooms, much less return to the ballroom without guidance.

Henry and Vi were dancing when I got back. They hadn't missed me at all, and footmen were so usual to them that they never asked what he was doing with my music and toe slippers. He had insisted on carrying them for me, no doubt concerned over being seen with me if his hands were empty and mine, full.

To my delight, Henry and Vi paid close attention to me as I danced. I had a wonderful evening. It was after midnight when they left me at the door of the Rose Suite. Mother was in bed, but wide-awake.

"I cannot bear to shut my eyes," she said. "Everything is so very beautiful and in such exquisite taste. Where on earth have you been? I sent one of the footmen to the nursery for you, but he returned saying it was quite dark and empty."

"It was," I explained. "When Doctor Robert's children went to bed, Henry and Vi and I went to the ballroom. I've been practicing my dances. A stage is all built, with curtains which pull. There'll be footlights on tomorrow. They're not connected yet. Did they build the stage just for me?"

"Hardly," Mother said, smiling. "It is put up and taken down for amateur theatricals. There's to be a play tomorrow, or is it today? Happy birthday, Regina! How does it feel to be Sweet Sixteen?"

"I've been kissed," I added. "Mr. Best and the Baron and some boy at Oxford whose name I don't know."

"Really!" Mother looked surprised. "You are growing up."

The following morning we were awakened by a discreet tapping on the door. When I opened it, a handsome damask-covered table was wheeled in by a footman. A heavy silver teapot, pitcher, creamer, sugar bowl, and great silver domes led us to expect a smashing breakfast, but we could discover nothing at all to eat except golden tea and four lace-like squares of bread and butter.

"We'll starve to death," Mother muttered as she sipped her tea and put a whole slice of bread into her mouth. "There must be a hundred pounds worth of silver here, but not an ounce of good solid food."

Our breakfast was out of the way in three minutes. Having nothing else to do, we finally dressed and went downstairs. Voices from the dining room and a footman's gloved hand pointing the way at the foot of the stairs soon solved the "light" breakfast problem. Breakfast hadn't been sent up, rather was it early-morning tea, for here was breakfast. Eggs, any way you chose, kippered herring, little sausages sizzling in chafing dishes, fruit, hot bread, tea, coffee, crumpets. The supply seemed inexhaustible. Neither Vi nor Henry were there, and suddenly I realized that very likely I shouldn't be, either.

"Mother!" I said, suddenly losing my appetite. "I ought to be in the nursery."

"You ought to be where?" Mother asked in surprise as Dr. Robert came toward us. Mother told him that today was my birthday, that I was all of sixteen. He beamed paternally. "Come to the library," he said. "I always see the girls there for a few moments before I go to work. Then you can run off and play."

Before I could say I was too old to play with the children, Mother told him I was to dance at the ball. She talked on, saying I hoped to become a professional dancer. He nodded courteously, looking only a little confused. In the library the girls were waiting. They kissed and hugged him politely. Then, when he went to the long glass-covered cases holding his beautifully arranged Egyptian treasures, everyone stood quietly as he explained them to us. He opened the cases and let us handle some of the pieces. Just before he shut the last one, he lifted out a greenish-colored necklace and laid it in my hands. "For a sixteenth birthday present," he told me, and kissed my forehead.

"Now, run along," he told the children. I handed the necklace to my mother, repeated my words of thanks, curtsied, and went off with the two girls. We spent an hour cleaning and dusting the dollhouse and watering the flowers. Then Vi and Henry arrived, and with one accord, we hurried off to the ballroom.

The footlights worked. The curtains worked, the portable dressing rooms had been set up. An accompanist had arrived, and in a few moments Mother appeared, saying Mrs. Ludwig Mond wanted to see me. I went to her sitting room, and she gave me a three-strand pearl necklace and bracelet. "It is not real, of course," she told me, "but I wore it when I was presented at Court. I thought you might like it. My grandchildren would not want it. They will have real pearls."

She was so pleased with my enthusiasm that she sent her

secretary to her jewel box and presented me with a turquoise-and-brilliant bracelet. "My favorite bit of jewelry," she told me. I often think it is mine. It brings back such happy memories when I look at it. What she called my "real" present was a blue leather gold-tooled writing case. Brand new, with my initials on it, it meant forethought and loving kindness. She then asked about my dances, if my costumes pleased me, and added that she had engaged an accompanist for me. He would be here all the time I was visiting so that I might practice as much as I pleased.

"Isn't she kind and thoughtful?" I asked, and Mother nodded. "She must always have been that way," she added. "Grandma often said it was her understanding and selflessness that made her such a wonderful wife to Ludwig, and may even have made his scientific career possible."

I practiced all day long. Just before dinner a footman brought a note from Mrs. Mond saying that Henry, Vi, and I were invited to have dessert at the adult dinner table.

"How wonderful!" I sighed in anticipation. Vi and Henry shrugged. It was no treat to them to dress up, help themselves to an ice held by a footman, sit quietly at the table, answering when spoken to, then leave unostentatiously when the ladies left the gentlemen to their liqueurs and cigars.

This dinner was a little different, for Sir Alfred proposed my good health in a toast and, having drunk it, came round to my place at the table and presented me with a dainty little brooch of white enamel set with tiny sapphires and pearls. Dr. Robert rose next, proposed a toast to my success, and came to my side and presented me with a gold bar-pin set with a single sapphire. When Lady Violet's rising gave the signal for the ladies to retire, we young people melted away. I took my presents to my room and, undressing, lay down on the couch as I had been told to do.

125

At eleven Mother appeared. I was still wide-eyed.

"Is it time?"

Mother nodded. "You can put the military uniform on here," she decided. "Mrs. Mond says you'll have all the time you want for changes. She's engaged a young man to do musical monologues and keep people from feeling bored."

"I know," I said. "I met him while we were all rehearsing. He's ever so funny."

"You sound very English." Mother smoothed my cape and handed me my hat. "Am I to dress you?"

"No. Mrs. Mond's maid is going to do that. She said she'd like to. You can sit and watch."

"Dear me, I'm getting so nervous." Mother patted the beads of perspiration on her forehead with a lace handkerchief. "Of course I shouldn't let you know. I should stay cool, calm, and collected. I'm a very bad example for you."

"No, you're not," I contradicted. "Seeing you scared makes me feel less stupid being so scared myself; but there's not much point in being scared, is there? This is what I wanted. If I don't really like it in front of an audience, I could go home, couldn't I?"

"Go home?" Mother took me in her arms. "You certainly could. I want you to live your life exactly as you want to live it, and so does your father. At home or abroad. In the theater or out of it. It is for you to decide."

"Thank you, Mother." I put my cheek against hers for a moment. "Let's go," I said, and led the way boldly. By now I knew the shortest route to the ballroom better than anyone else.

Dancing had a dreamlike quality. I heard my music. I danced. I saw the audience. I heard the applause. I bowed. My *Ballet Examination* received continued applause, and though neither my accompanist nor I had arranged for an encore, I was able to pick it up when he started to play again.

The basket of flowers passed me over the footlights was a complete surprise, and made my bliss complete.

I stayed in costume and went forward to be complimented and praised. It was a heady evening indeed, for I heard over and over again that I had unusual talent.

Back in our suite we had chicken sandwiches and milk. Mother was very quiet.

"Is there anything wrong, Mother?" I asked finally.

"No, dear," she said gently. "It's just that I'm a little surprised. I guess I've been counting on going home soon, but you're a better dancer than I dreamed you were, or ever could be. I guess we'll have to see it through, that is if you still want to be professional and like dancing before people."

"I love it," I said. "I just love it. Now I have to work very hard and try to dance really well. There's so much I don't know." I sighed.

"Don't worry, dear," Mother said brightly. "You've made a good start. I'm proud of you, and I know your father will be, too, when I write him how well you danced tonight."

chapter 12:   *Charity Concerts*

THE NEXT MORNING I slept late. I didn't hear our early-morning tea brought in, and Mother had already dressed and gone down to breakfast. I didn't feel particularly elated over my success the previous night. As I bathed and dressed slowly, two things kept nagging at me. Mr. D'Auban had said I had made three years' progress in four months, but all of it, I knew he thought, was due to my years of study in the Dalcroze method of gymnastics. He assumed this preparatory work was what had made it possible for me to assimilate and do steps far beyond any natural ability or aptitude.

"You won't be able to coast any more on what you've learned," he'd explained. "You've used up all your reserve. From now on, you'll be just like any other dancer. Your love for dance and your passionate dedication to it will be challenged by many others far more beautiful, far better trained, a few far less scrupulous, but all dedicated to making success an end in itself."

I hadn't paid too much attention to his lecture, preferring to bask in the memory of the day he had said I was kin to Maria Taglioni in my naturally good *ballon*. However, his words of warning crowded in on Mother's decision that maybe I really would have to be evaluated once more by Mr. Stuart the coming August. What then? I didn't know. Home or abroad, I supposed, but in January, August sounded light-years away. I counted off the months on my fingers. Really, only eight months! I would have to work very hard. Could I, by some miracle, make each month count as one year? I didn't know, but I could try.

I resolved that nothing from now on should interfere with my training and practice, nothing at all.

Luck was with me. Now that the party was over, many house guests were going on to other parties or back home to more prosaic duties. Mrs. Ludwig Mond was returning to her town house, Sir Alfred and Lady Violet were going to Egypt, as was Dr. Robert. Mother met Mrs. Mond's secretary in the hall, and somehow an invitation was issued for us to drive back to London that very morning. I was summoned from the lovely dollhouse where all of us children were sitting dispiritedly wondering what to do next after the exciting events of our holiday.

Mother had almost finished packing when I got back to our suite. "Will you mind very much?" she asked, folding blouses rapidly. "Everyone is off somewhere, and I thought I'd like to get back to the picture galleries, and I suppose you'll want to get back to your lessons. When will the schools open again?"

"Mother!" I sat on a suitcase in answer to an imperative gesture. "Professional schools never close. I bet some of the kids were practicing on Christmas Day."

"Dear me." Mother yanked triumphantly at a strap. "How odd; but going back to London is all right with you?"

"Oh, yes." I gave a little sigh. "I have to get back to work. I have so much to learn."

The ride back to London was swift and effortless. Mrs. Mond said little, and we spoke only when spoken to. She was nearly eighty and in delicate health. We knew that parting with her sons and grandchildren, even if only for a few months, was a serious business. At Carlton Mansions I kissed her cheek and thanked her for the Christmas holiday. She smiled gently and said she would get in touch with us.

We let ourselves in and carried our bags up the stairs. Happily, our rooms were empty of their previous tenants. We settled in. I practiced. We spoke briefly at supper of our wonderful visit. Mother sat for a while in the living room and visited with the guests she knew. I was in a quietly depressed mood. Doubt of my own ability and doubt of the possibility of ever achieving my goal as a professional dancer filled me with gloom.

Back at Mr. D'Auban's enthusiasm again ran in my veins. I danced my dances over for him and explained the mistakes I had made in performance. First of all, I told him, the transitions from one step to another had been very poor. I felt I had done them badly and that every step showed where it began and where it ended. What was even more aggravating was that I had had to sacrifice height in both my *arabesques* and my extensions because I was not steady on my feet. It was very embarrassing. I actually danced better here in the classroom than I had for an audience. What was the matter with me? He let me talk until I ran down. When I sat on the floor, too tired and weary to do anything but listen, he began to speak.

"You are ready now to work seriously," he told me, "for you see yourself as you really are, not as you have imagined yourself to be. You must stop pressing and strive only for perfection in everything you do. Put your silly costumes away in sheets. From now on you must concentrate on exercises and adagios. Except for a charity concert or two, you won't dance again in public until you are in rehearsal for some professional engagement. You are at a point now where if you spend your time on the small things, the big ones will take care of themselves."

"You mean height and easy transition . . ."

"Height will come from carefully exercised muscles, a very little at a time over a period of months and years. A transition between steps is nothing but the ability to do each step so well that one flows into the other without conscious thought or effort."

At Zanfretta's I found myself moving less violently and spending a great deal of time merely attempting to perfect the way I looked in the mirror when I was standing still in various positions. Everything about me I eyed critically, from the tilt of my head to the angle of my feet. Knees, shoulders, hips I looked at in disdain. They were so far from the meticulously perfect placing of the great ballerinas I venerated that I might well be a poorly jointed cheap doll. I made horrible faces in the mirror to show my contempt for myself.

Madame did not share my disgust. "You eemprove." She patted my shoulder. "Slowlee, slowlee, duz eet." And with a few deft shakes, as if I were filled with sawdust, she contrived to make me look like a good ballerina. "Feel eet," she told me. "You mus' feel eet, in the way the bones set, the way the muscles pull."

I stood motionless, trying to analyze what she had done that I had never done before. That day she called me to her. "You mus' stop working so hard to get the height. What you mus' do is practice, practice the adagio. Very slowlee,

131

very, very slowlee. Stop trying to do everything so beeg. Do it small, but quite pairfecte."

"Yes, Madame," I said, and went into the dressing room. I wasn't conscious of the girls, whether they spoke to me or not, or what they were talking about. I only know that for the first time after a lesson at Mme. Zanfretta's we went downstairs together, had a cup of tea at a Lyons and parted at the bus stop, their good-bys ringing in my ears.

"So long, don't strain a muscle; far better to strain your mind."

"Be good and you'll be lonesome."

" 'By now, Jinny."

I was on the bus and in my seat on the open deck before I realized that I was one of them, not an outsider, not teacher's pet, not someone called "Amerika," but a girl they called Jinny, who went to tea with them and said good-by at the bus stop.

It didn't seem possible. I didn't know it was a milestone then, but I was changed. I had changed from a dilettante to a worker, from an outsider to an insider, from a girl who liked to dance to a dancer who liked to learn.

At home I was less bouncy and exuberant and found myself included in many of the adult groups at tea and after-dinner coffee. I was learning to listen, and found the listening both stimulating and rewarding. Mother began to stay to watch me practice. No longer was I trying to turn myself inside out. Our visits to the museums were now more comradely. I tried to see what she saw in paintings and statues and was rewarded by an inner light of understanding. Now when I tried to re-create a pose, it came far more easily.

I worked longer hours, but I was under less pressure. Since I was trying for perfection, I was working much more carefully. I did more thinking about what I was trying to accomplish, and when I succeeded a little bit, I felt peaceful and grateful instead of excited and weary.

The months went by, one day almost exactly like another. I went to my lessons, I practiced; we went to church and to tea on Sunday. I went to a ballet one or two evenings a week, but the theater was not part of my normal life. I no longer tried to do what the great ones did, but to do what my teachers told me to do.

I was busy, happy as only a vegetable or a student can be when growing or learning is their only business. The spring holiday came late in April, and we spent a few days at Felixstowe. I rode horseback on the beach in the mornings, practiced, and slept in the afternoons and danced at a charity concert in the evening when I was asked. Not having made any arrangement about money, Mother was delighted to find a whole guinea, in an envelope with my name on it, in the rack at the door after one performance.

"A guinea." Mother smiled. "How very nice to be paid in guineas! Doesn't it make you feel exclusive and aristocratic?"

"One guinea!" I corrected. "But it'll buy two pairs of toe shoes, and how I need them!"

We spent one day coaching in the low country around Felixstowe, but this time I found the trip noisy, dusty, and tiresome. It took time I should have spent on practice, and I was moody and most unco-operative.

At the pension I found a letter waiting. I was uncertain whether to be annoyed or thrilled. An open-air lawn fete offered me two pounds (not guineas) to appear that evening when the moon was full and just coming over the trees.

"When is the moon full?" I demanded of the elderly room clerk.

"Full of what?" He cupped his hand around his ear.

133

"Light, I suppose," I shouted. "When does the moon come up?"

"At night!" He settled back and picked up his paper. " 'Most night now. Why not go out and have a look?"

"The sun hasn't set," I yelled. "I can't even see the moon."

He shook his head sadly. "Too bad. Better get glasses." He resumed his reading, setting his eyeglasses more firmly on his nose. I yearned to shake him. There was an imperceptible smile on his lips, and I was practically certain he was pulling my leg. I had an idea he was no deafer than I was, but used the dodge to confuse and irritate the borders with his aptly inapt answers.

"The moon rises about nine-ten," an elderly lady told me as I left the desk. "I saw it from my window last night about half past eight. It will be in the paper. There's one on the sofa over there."

I thanked her and went out to the veranda, where my mother was sitting, discussing the day. I showed her the letter, pointing out that my fee would be in pounds, not guineas.

"Two pounds is far better than one guinea," Mother announced, "but what will you wear? It says 'soft draperies on the order of Isadora Duncan,' and what will you dance? You have no such dance in your repertoire, have you?"

"I'll wear a pink leotard and you'll sew and pin my new pink scarf on it. I'll be barefoot, and I'll wave the beautiful pink and silver material Mrs. Mond gave you for a new evening dress. I shan't really dance—I couldn't, on a lawn. I'll float around and pose."

Mother moaned. "My pink and silver material! It'll be ruined."

"No, it won't. I'll be very careful."

A note of acceptance was dispatched, along with a request for slow, dreamy violin music. Mother found the pink scarf

would not mold to my body, so she heroically cut up the
lovely material Mrs. Mond had given her for Christmas and
tacked a yard and a half of it to my leotard in the style of
Isadora Duncan's draperies. Then Mother bound the material tight under my breasts with a bit of silver ribbon from
a candy box. I combed my hair out, and Mother curled the
ends loosely with her pocket curling-iron, which she heated
over a small alcohol stove. I put on an Alice in Wonderland
comb, one of my Christmas presents, and Mother announced
that I looked just lovely. Over my costume she placed a
silken shawl. I slipped my feet into black patent leather
slippers and we started off in a smelly hack for the lawn fete.

Once arrived, I was instantly hidden in the gypsy fortune-
teller's tent. I listened to a dozen fortunes, but never my
own. I watched the sky anxiously from a slit in the tent,
which somehow kept getting larger and larger as I peered
this way and that, searching for the rise of the moon which
would be my cue to dance. When it did, it rose on the other
side of the tent, and I never saw it at all until an imposing
heavy-set lady in a flowered chiffon dress and flowered toque
descended upon me, hissed furiously that I was "shockingly
late," pushed me into some bushes, and disappeared.

My first obligation seemed to be to find the audience,
locate the greensward upon which to dance, and hope to
heaven that I could hear the music. Faint chirrups indicated
either poorly tuned violins or asthmatic crickets. I peered
about, saw lights ahead, playing spasmodically on a square
of ground, and a number of people standing with their backs
to it. There was nowhere else to dance; the music, if it was
music, piped drearily. I unfolded Mother's new evening-dress
material. It floated in heavenly fashion above me as I ran
toward the light and my unresponsive audience.

The grass was deep, harsh to the feet, the ground
humocky. Speed was impossible, *ballon* unimaginable. I

135

moved as gracefully as I could when one moment I was knee deep in grass, the next, balanced on an oddly shaped mushroom of earth. I moved about, swayed, waved my scarf, lifted a leg or an arm high in the air, sank to the ground and rose again to run reasonably lightly, I hoped, about the pseudo-stage. Most of those people whose backs were presented to me turned, looked at me in polite surprise, and looked away again. I was causing not a ripple of interest, and I was frightfully annoyed. And then there burst on the air a blast of noise, the like of which I'd never heard. It was a German brass band braying forth "Shine, Little Glowworm" for all it was worth.

A man galloped toward me. "Miss! Miss!" He caught my hand. "You must stop practicing at once and come dance."

Speechless, I allowed myself to be led through the crowd. Practicing! The fool! I had just finished dancing. On the other side of the crowd I found my audience, sitting in wire chairs drawn up in neat rows. The moon was just over the trees, the grass was as smoothly shaved as a newly covered billiard table. The band, in uniform, was bellowing mightily. As I appeared, a perfunctory patter of applause greeted me. The flowered lady bore down on me.

"You are supposed to appear from the shrubbery!" She rolled her r's and sizzled her s's. I knew at once that whatever shrubbery I had been lurking in was the wrong shrubbery, or else I had chosen the wrong direction from which to appear. Hastily I was again hidden from the patient audience, and after a few sour brays from the band, the melody of the even-then hackneyed "Glowworm" caused me to leap forth.

The first time I had danced that evening I had to contend with odd chirruping sounds, a rough bit of pastureland, and a completely uninterested audience. Now I had music so

136

insistent, so noisy, I couldn't hear myself think, a perfect piece of greensward to dance on, and what seemed to me hundreds of intent spectators.

At first I moved, trancelike, frightened to death and so tired from giving my all to nobody in particular that I couldn't get my breath. Once, on a turn, I got a glimpse of beautiful dark trees massed against a blue-black sky with a resplendent orange moon hanging just above them. It was then that the scene the audience was seeing became clear to me. I moved backward and merged myself with the beauty of the night, and forgetting the banality of the music, attempted only to be part and parcel of the natural loveliness of which I had so recently become aware. Now I moved swiftly from side to side, in diagonals, in circles. My scarf floated, my legs rose in *arabesques*; I did back bends, I sank to the ground and got my breath in prayerful reverent weavings. I turned my back on the audience and worshiped the moon's glowing glory. I sank to my knees. I bowed low, I rose, and bowing, hoping always that my bows looked reverent and not servile, I took refuge in the shrubbery.

I heard applause. I couldn't take a bow because I had backed into a bush and torn some of my draperies. I was trying to examine the damage done when I was collected by a small man in livery.

"Very nice indeed, Miss," he said. "Please follow me. Mrs. Masterwollingood wishes to speak with you."

The lady of the flowered toque breathed hard and said my performance was "quite decent for an American. Don't care for such goings-on, myself," she told me. "I'm one for Adeline Genée now, but a person can't expect a Genée for two pounds. Here's your money, m'dear. Do whatever you did again, say in twenty minutes. Have an ice with your dear mother, after, and enjoy the fair. Thank you *so* much."

Mother came and pinned me together as best she could,

warning me to drape my scarf about me when I stood with my back to the audience.

"It's higher now," she pointed to the moon. "Couldn't you worship it facing the audience? It'd be a whole lot safer. There's a tear in your leotard right where you sit down."

"Oh, Mom!" But there was no time to say more, for the strains of "Shine Little Glowworm" were already filling the air. Now that I knew where the audience was, where the stage was, where the musicians were and where the moon was likely to be, dancing was much easier. I rather enjoyed turning, wrapping myself in my scarf and doing an *arabesque* with the leg with the torn leotard lifted high, thus obscuring the tear. I dropped to my knees, my back to the audience but safely hidden from view by my lovely scarf. I bowed myself off sideways and backed into Mother's protecting arms.

"I expect it was all right from the front," she consoled me, "but from here . . ."

I knew what she meant when I put my hand back. "Heavens! I'm quite bare."

Mother chuckled. "Lucky you danced by the light of the moon and not floodlights or you'd have been run in by the local police. Did you get your money?"

I nodded and pulled it out of my chest. Wrapped in my shawl, I faced the world, chin up, a smile on my lips. We had pink ices, but I suddenly felt cold. "Let's go home," I said. "I feel perfectly silly in this getup. I'd like to go back to London right away and get to work. I'm tired of holidays."

"So am I," Mother agreed. "We'll go tomorrow. At that, the best part of a holiday is the unpacking once you're home again."

chapter 13:   *The Year's End*

DAY FOLLOWED DAY in routine fashion. I continued to dance at charity fetes, once at the Fourth of July reception at the American Embassy. We met hundreds of Americans, most of them tourists, some of them music and voice students. I seemed more or less a freak. Whoever heard of an American girl studying dancing? And if I was going to study dancing, why London? Didn't I know London was famous only for its kings and queens, its crown jewels, its roast beef and its pea-soup fogs? London wasn't artistic, and dancing was at a very low ebb anyway.

"I dance, and I don't get a penny for it, and then a lot of horrible people say dancing is at a low ebb," I fumed as I dressed. "I suppose my dancing is the lowest ebb they can imagine, but I'd rather they said I was lousy than just confuse me with the tides."

"Don't be childish," Mother said briskly. "It's of no importance. I expect they're just jealous you were asked to perform and their daughters weren't. You danced very nicely."

"Tide's turning." I managed a bleak smile. "Let's get away."

"First you must say good-by. I believe the Ambassador has gone to his study. Stop in there," Mother told me. "He said he wished to see you before you left."

"Oh, all right." I followed the manservant, who knocked discreetly on the paneled door.

The Ambassador was sitting at his desk. He turned, smiled cordially. "A lovely performance," he told me. "Here is a letter of introduction to Mr. Herrick in Paris. Your mother says you may be going abroad for a short vacation. And then I want to give you this." He presented me with a five-pound box of Page and Shaw's candies. "Direct from the U.S.A.," he said. "And here is a little bangle." He clasped a silver bracelet about my wrist. There were several charms on it, room for many more. "Be sure and come back and see us after you are famous. Good luck and our blessing."

I stammered my thanks, blushing even redder than the roses wrapped up and waiting for me at the entrance.

"I feel so cheap," I told Mother. "There I was yapping about how mean everyone was, and just look, the Ambassador himself complimented me and gave me candy and flowers and a silver bracelet and a letter of introduction to the Ambassador in Paris."

"How wonderful," Mother said. "You should be very happy." I nodded. But my London year was ending, and I was beginning to be afraid. A trip to Paris, a little vacation trip, might well mean that we would soon be headed home. After all, I'd had a year of lessons in London. By now I knew that nine out of ten girls wanted to dance professionally, and I had come to realize that of the nine girls who wanted to dance, nine of them were better looking and better dancers than I was. It really was time I stopped fooling myself. Technically I was pretty good, I loved to dance, and I enjoyed working, but I had no unusual array of talents with which to buck the professional dance world.

Letters came from Father quite regularly. We were frightened when we saw a Bermuda postmark, but the news wasn't as bad as we feared. The mortgage on the house was paid, he had sold some land in St. Paul. He had caught a bad cold. The cough hung on, and Dr. Hinckley had suggested Bermuda. So there he was, most comfortably settled in his favorite spot. He wrote, "My cough is gone. I walk in the sunshine and drink in the salty air. Passionflowers will soon be in bloom. I think of you often. . . ."

Mr. D'Auban was planning my dances for my audition at the Gaiety. One day he reared back on his heels, stopped playing, and asked, "If you were going to dance what you pleased for Mr. Stuart, what would it be?"

I thought a moment. It was something I'd been wondering about for weeks. The dances Mr. D'Auban was planning seemed too slick and machine made. I felt like an automaton as I danced them, and the better I danced, the more imprisoned I felt.

"I expect I'd like to do the kind of dance I thought I was doing when I auditioned the first time," I said slowly. "Something fresh and lovely and lyric."

"That's what it should be," he agreed. "What music? I'll play it for you." We tried a dozen pieces before we finally agreed on one.

"I'm ready," I told him, and waited for him to tell me what to do. He just played. He was smiling.

"It's your dance," he told me. "Get on with it. I'm just your accompanist."

Of course I didn't do it all myself, though I did plan, shape, and form to some extent. It was he who smoothed and cleaned up the pattern, who pulled my original composition into shape.

"Now something dramatic," he ordered, and once again we went to work. The weeks slid by in rehearsal and practice. Mother was making plans.

"I should think, even if you have to have another six months' work here in London, that we could take a Cook's tour to Paris. Nine days wouldn't be too expensive, and it would make a nice little change, wouldn't it?"

I nodded mutely; I knew Mother wanted to see the Louvre and the Luxembourg before we returned to the States. I did too, in a way, but even more I wanted to see the Paris Opera Ballet, to study there, to have some French and Italian ballet training. I feared my audition with Mr. Stuart. I feared that "little vacation trip." Both presaged in my mind the ominous possibility of going home, just another little American girl who had studied abroad. She hadn't exactly failed, for she'd never even started professionally: she had just been a nice ladylike social success, with an occasional guinea flung her way as a sop to conventions.

The night before my audition I lay silently in my bed, too frightened even to speak. At my request, Mother had made me a very simple pink practice frock. I had new ballet shoes, carefully broken in under old silk stockings to keep them clean. I was certain Mr. Stuart would be interested in how much I'd improved, how I'd changed, and what possibilities, if any, lay ahead of me. I suspected that costumer-costumes, make-up, or any attempt at glamor would spoil my chances completely. I told Mother I wanted to go alone, just as I'd gone the first time. She agreed. I started at break of day. I was so nervous, I nearly got myself run over, and even then was so early that I cooled my heels pacing up and down the sidewalk outside the theater until the doorman ordered me in because I made him dizzy.

Mr. Stuart stalked in, looked at me once or twice, said, "Hello there, you've changed quite a bit. Want a dressing room, or will you change behind a flat?"

"A dressing room," I said primly. When I had changed, I came out with my music. I put it on the stand and stood, waiting, doing a few *barre* exercises to warm up as unobtrusively as possible. Mr. Stuart was talking with several men and one woman. Suddenly the woman came to the piano, opened my music, and began to play.

"Time?" she asked, and I gave her the beat. "This one first, please." I changed the dramatic dance to the lyric one. She looked at Mr. Stuart. He nodded. She looked at me. I took my position. This was it. All I could do was my best.

She played well. Each step came smoothly. I was content that the transitions were almost invisible. My dance flowed effortlessly. When it was over, I looked to Mr. Stuart, not for approval, but for permission to go on.

"Get your breath," he said, and began to talk to the men beside him. I knew he wasn't talking about me. A few moments later he caught the accompanist's eye. She looked at me. I smiled, with stiff lips.

This dance had all my repressed love of dramatic and lyric dancing in it. I forgot I was auditioning, I forgot it was a dance I'd learned and practiced and agonized over. I danced for sheer absolute joy. When it was over, it was hard to pull myself back into the present. I hated to come back to earth and the prosaic everyday plans an aspiring dancer must make.

Mr. Stuart motioned me to come to him. "You have improved beyond my expectations," he said. "Come to tea this afternoon at five. Bring your mother. I must think a little. I was not quite prepared for what you have shown me.

143

I had thought of a chorus job, an understudy role here, but now I don't know. Perhaps you should study a little longer."

My report to my mother was incoherent. "He said I was quite different from what he had expected and that maybe I had better study some more, but he did say I'd improved a whole lot."

"Improved!" Mother was exasperated. "I should hope so. But what I want to know is when you will be good enough to dance in public. I shall ask him point-blank—when? Then we'll see."

"I'm afraid I'm a very slow learner," I apologized. "I'm sorry."

Mother sniffed, but she didn't look a bit cross.

At five o'clock we were once again in Mr. Stuart's drawing room at Russell Square. This time I was dressed simply in schoolgirl navy blue, white blouse, and low heels. Mr. Stuart smiled as Mother demanded his unequivocal opinion.

"She's changed a lot, Mrs. Jones," he said, sipping his tea. "She dances extremely well, and she gives me the impression of leashed power and a very unusual quality of projection. She may be going to be quite good. There are several partial scholarships available for study in Paris with Dorenio, Stichel, and Leo Staats. If you can support yourselves over there, I shall be happy to recommend her to these teachers."

"Paris!" Mother looked startled. "How long will she have to study?"

"No one can know that for sure, because if she is a really dedicated dancer, she won't stop learning until the breath leaves her body," he said softly. "But I would say that by springtime you will know if she is ready for a professional debut. It shouldn't be too hard, either. Paris is unusually receptive to lovely young American girls. Isadora Duncan is idolized, as you know."

"Isadora Duncan is a genius," Mother said. "But we will

go to Paris and try our luck. You think that is better than staying here?"

"Yes, I do. Your daughter, if I may say so, is considerably more the continental type of dancer than the English."

"Was that supposed to be a compliment?" Mother fretted later, "or was it a brush-off?"

I didn't know. I didn't much care. Six months in Paris, with lessons within our means and still perhaps enough time to do some sight-seeing!

Saying good-by to London was heartbreaking. We had made so many friends. I'd grown so used to my classes that my good-bys were made tearfully. I'm not sure I'd have really gone if Mr. Best hadn't suddenly appeared from the States full of news of my father, our Boston friends, and bubbling over at the idea of my spending the winter in Paris.

"But first," he cried. "You both must have a holiday. What say to a quick trip to Holland? I have to go over on business. You can do it on a Cook's tour, and we'll meet now and then. I'll take you to dinner and you can see Rembrandt's 'The Night Watch.' Wonderful, wonderful painting. Let's lunch at Selfridge's and talk it over."

Once again I was swept along on a breathless sight-seeing tour, but first I had to go and say good-by to Mrs. Mond. It was the last time I saw her. She smiled and listened to my plans, asking many interested questions. Before I left, she gave me a lovely jewel case filled with trinkets. "Paste of course," she explained, "but they may be of use in the theater."

She kissed me good-by and wished me God speed.

Leaving London, which had been our home for so long, was momentous and slightly awe-inspiring. Paris would be thrilling and exciting, but London was so beloved, so familiar, that we were lonesome before we left.

The trip across the Channel was perfect. The sun shone,

the water was glassy-blue and smooth. That no food was served on the boat proved an unwelcome surprise. By the time we reached The Hague we were starved. Cheese and rusks and golden-brown coffee was the most unusual breakfast we ever ate, but it tasted good, as we were ravenous.

The Dutch people were kindly and courteous. We loved the countryside, and Mother was enchanted with the silver buttons on the trousers of the Volendam men.

"I suppose they hold their trousers up," she told me, "but how I would like to buy those buttons."

Windmills turned slowly, sitting in flat fields of flowers. Surprisingly, they were pansies rather than tulips, but there were so many of them, they made colorful carpets as far as the eye could see.

"The Night Watch" hung in a dark room with curtains drawn over it. When they were swept back to reveal the picture, it was theatrically effective. Mother sat in rapt contemplation before it. To me, it was just another painting.

A fine dinner, a ride on a barge on the biggest canal, and Mr. Best put us on a train for Paris. My eyes were misty with unshed tears. I hated to say good-by. Success might lie ahead, but it seemed then as if all my friends and everything we loved were being left behind.

chapter 14:   Paris

PARIS WAS beautiful, lonely, and very expensive. We lived in a small hotel filled with American tourists who seemed strange and noisy and took us for English tourists. We would have laughed if they hadn't been so rude and insulting.

We visited the Left Bank. Mother was not impressed. "They are very queer people," she told me. "I couldn't be happy here. It's dirty, there are bugs and horrible smells."

"There are also lots of Americans," I pointed out. "You don't speak French very well. It might keep you from being lonesome."

"I prefer being lonesome to listening to those women talk about their daughters' voices," she said. "Everyone of them insists *her* daughter is better than Jenny Lind, Galli-Curci, and Tetrazzini."

"You wouldn't brag, would you?" I asked, and was surprised at her serious answer.

"They're not just bragging, they say mean things about dancers. They say nice girls don't take up ballet."

"W-why . . ." I stammered in my surprise.

"Let's stop trying to find a place to board and get a little apartment near the Opera," Mother suggested. "I'd like to cook a little. We could get our own breakfast and dinners. We'll both be out at lunchtime. It would save a lot of money."

The idea delighted us. We bought newspapers and scanned the advertisements, and to our surprise and everlasting enchantment, found on the top floor of a small hotel on the rue de Helder, a two-room penthouse apartment. Six flights by slow *ascenseur*, then one flight on foot, and there we were, high in the air, only a few hundred feet from the Opera House, with a quarter-acre terrace all our own. The penthouse had been built for the manager of the hotel, but it was inconvenient for him. The usual hotel guests balked at the extra flight, and the manager himself had misgivings about renting it except to rather settled folk.

"It could be quite *dangereux*," he explained. "There is no rail. If one should drink a little too much, and perhaps *tombe*, it would give the hotel a bad name."

We assured him that we never drank, that we would be careful not to fall off his roof, that we would make our own beds. I am certain we would have promised him anything he asked for, for the price of the rooms was within our means, they were light, clean, and airy, and in the very heart of Paris. He accepted us as tenants once it was made clear that I was not a singer. American voices, he explained seriously, gave him a dreadful *mal à la tête*. It was hard for him to believe I was a danseuse, so I gave an impromptu performance on the roof, explained that I hoped to study with Leo Staats, ballet master of the Paris Opera, and immediately we were signed in as tenants. He was as happy to have a danseuse in the house as our American compatriots had been suspicious.

We unpacked and went into a huddle over our finances. Paris was going to cost considerably more than London. After paying the rent, we decided we could afford $10 a week for my lessons. We'd have to spend $15 or $20 a week for food, and allow at least $10 for miscellaneous items. No more taxis or restaurant meals. As for museums, we'd go only when they were free.

Sighing a little over our restricted budget, Mother went off to the Louvre and I, to present my letters. I had thought to see all the teachers before I made a choice, but M. Staats was in the provinces and Madame Stichel was home ill. Only M. Dorenio was left. I found him to be a handsome, harried, excitable man who had a studio full of pupils. He watched me dance and accepted me for three lessons a week at ten dollars. But nothing I did suited him. He placed me at the *barre* and quarreled with every movement I made. He said I wasn't ready for unsupported adagio and kept me doing *pliés* and back bends till I was bored stiff. I stuck it out for two weeks. Then during the second lesson of the third week, just after I'd paid him, I left the floor, dressed, and walked out of the studio, never to return. I had rebelled more at what he had said to someone else than to me, though I felt sure it applied.

"There is only *one* right way," he shouted, banging his cane on the floor. "*I* tell you what it is. *You* do it. No arguments. *Voyons. Un, deux, trois!*"

"Only one way, and *he* knows it," I told myself. Impossible to work with such a conceited egotist. Suddenly I knew I must meet Madame Stichel and M. Staats. If they

149

were unavailable or like M. Dorenio, I would go straight back to London. If they were nice . . . I shrugged and got on a bus.

I found Madame Stichel quite recovered and teaching class. She was Italian. Slim, gentle, very sincere. I liked the way her students danced. They were well trained and they looked happy. She read my note from England. She watched my audition politely. She listened to my explanation of my restricted budget. Finally she said, "But of course you may come every morning and stay as long as you wish. Have no fear, little one," she told me. "You shall dance as much as you please for your five *dollar*."

Next I called on M. Staats. He was just back from the provinces. Handsome, dark, very young to be ballet master at the Opera, he accepted me as a pupil, two lessons a week for whatever I could afford to pay, which was, of course, five dollars. He, too, gave me permission to watch as long as I liked when my own classes were over.

The week's end found me happily ensconced in both schools. Madame Stichel was a magnificent teacher. She loved and taught the strong, brilliant athletic type of ballet in which the Italians specialize, and I found her love of *ballon* quite equal to my own. She liked my dancing and she liked me. I loved her. My mornings were full, happy ones. Soon she suggested we lunch together, and it was she who insisted that two fresh eggs be poached in my clear chicken broth. With this I ate delicious slices of crusty French bread and finished up with a bit of creamy Camembert cheese.

From the Étoile Palace, where she held her classes, I went directly to M. Staats's studio. Whether I was watching or dancing, I changed into practice costume and slippers. This may have confused M. Staats, though it is more likely he really didn't care whether I took two lessons or six for my twenty francs. I myself was meticulous about it. I never went on the floor except on Tuesday and Thursdays. However, if I was asked why I was "sitting down like a lazy lump instead of dancing," I always rose and began to dance, for I considered my duty done. I then proceeded to get as much out of the unexpected lesson as possible.

Being small, even if I started in the back row, I was usually brought forward. I found M. Staats a fascinating teacher, a generous, kindly person and a connoisseur of dance. His students seemed truly superior dancers. They were supple, graceful, and beautifully turned out. They moved with varying degrees of ability, but he seemed as anxious to retain the personal quality of each dancer as M. Dorenio was determined to erase it.

Lessons with M. Staats were real workouts. He danced with us, never sparing himself, trying to get from us the kind of movement he believed we were capable of. We were never compared with one another, scolded, or mocked, and yet he managed to have each one of us always striving to do her very best. We vied with each other in the hope of a smile, a pat, or a word of praise.

Mother was entranced with the Louvre. "I could live there" she told me, and she meant it. I myself loved the Luxembourg. Paintings were her delight, but I got far more from a piece of sculpture than from a picture. She was very patient, however, and went wherever I wanted to go whenever I had the time.

Just as in London, we went to the ballet when free tickets were available. I watched Zambelli night after night, and marveled at her speed and grace. I still considered Tamara Karsavina the greatest technician I had ever seen, while Adeline Genée remained my ideal of an exquisite ballerina. Anna Pavlova was still my idol. She held my heart in her hands. For me she was the perfect ballerina. Mother did not go with me to the ballet after the first few nights.

"I'm sorry, dear," she told me, "but I just can't care about ballet dancing the way you do. The stairs exhaust me, and if I have to stand up, all I can think of is that my feet hurt."

"Your feet don't hurt in a picture gallery," I accused her.

"That is because my mind is occupied with the glorious paintings," she explained. "It cannot occupy itself with miniature people running about on a badly lit stage in dirty pink tights."

"The stage isn't badly lit, and the tights aren't dirty," I protested.

Mother looked smug. "It bores me," she said, and turned away to read one of my father's voluminous hand-written letters again. I knew she was lonesome, and strangely enough, I was, too. In London we had both been completely happy. It wasn't so here in Paris. We had as much, or more, but we didn't feel loved, cherished, or wanted.

I stuck doggedly to my lessons. I practiced. I went to the Opera. All morning I was with Madame Stichel. All afternoon, now, I was with M. Staats. Sometimes I danced, sometimes I merely watched, but always I was absorbing a great deal of knowledge about the dance.

At Christmastime a personal note from Ambassador Myron T. Herrick asked me to dance at the traditional reception for American tourists and expatriates. This was the beginning of our social life in Paris. I left the Embassy, my arms full of roses, new books, and candy. From that time on I performed at afternoon teas, at soirees, at parties. Sometimes I was paid well, in cash, in presents, in compliments. At other times I was treated as a servant, spoken to rudely, and given faded flowers as a gratuity. I never knew when I left home in a private car or a taxi whether I would be the princess in a fairy tale or Cinderella in her ashes.

The people I met at the teas, soirees, and dansants looked

a great deal like my English audiences, but they varied greatly in their behavior toward me. Whereas in London I had been looked upon as a charming child dancing for her supper and rewarded with a doll or a pat on the head, here I found myself fair game for the male sex. I soon realized that I could, as Mother put it, "trust nothing in pants," whether the pants were evening dress trousers or a footman's livery. Even my beloved bearded gentlemen no longer presaged safety.

"The old goat," Mother snapped after being soundly kissed in a corner.

"He pinched me," I wailed, and then Mother laughed.

"We are two sillies. Kissing and pinching are but part of the custom of this country in the kind of society in which we find ourselves. Frankly, my dear, we are in the wrong place. A female has no business complaining if she finds herself pinched when she has gone to great pains to dress and act the wanton."

"Why, Mother. How can you talk like that?" I demanded, deeply hurt. I even stopped packing my woodland nymph costume, which was based on Anna Pavlova's *Bacchanale* costume. I must admit that it didn't take up much room, but it was decent.

"Because it's the truth," Mother said. "We might as well face it. You're really nothing but a schoolgirl. But in costume and dancing you look like the most glamorous demi-mondaine. You dance provocatively, and your innocence seems both assumed and maddening."

"What on earth can I do about it?" I asked.

"Stop dancing," Mother answered.

"But I've just begun," I argued.

"I know." Mother picked up my cosmetic case. "Come along. We'll have to talk this out." At the door we were given an envelope. The footman called a cab. As we were entering, a tall dark man with a wavy lock of hair over one eye plunged down the steps, hatless.

"I must talk to you." He leaped in beside us without our assent. "My name is Brown-Smith," he told us, which I can assure you it wasn't. "To save trying to find your address and then coming to call, I take advantage of this opportunity to put a proposition to you."

"No propositions!" Mother said. "Get out, please."

"Madame. You misunderstand me." He looked injured. "This is a *business* proposition. My business is getting up unusual balls for wealthy people. I am doing one for Madame Rienzini for March tenth. It will be a gala evening of Indian and Hindu dancing, scenery, and food. We will have the very best. I have been hiring dancers and singers. Tonight Madame Rienzini saw you and ordered you to be included. She is a very rich American and must not be crossed, so here I am. Will you dance for her March tenth—really at two A.M. March eleventh?"

"I couldn't." I explained, "I do not know or like Indian dancing and I have no costume."

"Madame wants you," he repeated.

"I'm sorry. I can't."

He talked on and on. I reiterated my noes, and Mother backed me up. At home I put my costumes in the closet and prepared for bed. Mother came in and sat down.

"How about going home?" she asked. "This is no life for you or for me. I admit I see beautiful pictures all day. I enjoy going with you when you pose for Raphael Kirchner and for Louis Kronberg. Art fascinates me, but you look tired all the time, we do nothing but gad about, and you entertain at most of these parties for less than it costs us in time, effort, and money."

"I know," I agreed. "But everyone says I have to be seen before I get a professional job, and this is the only way."

"I suppose it is," she admitted, "but I'm getting home-sick."

"So am I," I told her, "but let me stay till July, when the summer shows are all cast and rehearsed. If I've nothing then——"

"We'll go to Vienna and Budapest, Munich and Brussels, and then home!" Mother interrupted. "We will call these two years a finishing-school education. You could teach dancing——"

"I couldn't and wouldn't!" I said heatedly. "I can dance, but I don't know enough to teach. My best bet is chore-ography. I like making up dances."

"Better go to bed now," Mother said wearily. "It's five minutes to four, and you've a lesson at nine."

It was good to get back to class. I enjoyed working at danc-ing. The studio was clean, and the dancing itself, always a fresh delight. I returned at five to find Mother cooking a delicious-smelling lamb stew on our one-burner electric plate.

"Mrs. Rienzini was here," Mother told me, beaming. "I told her you would dance. You will be given free lessons in Indian dancing by some Indian person, your costume—all jeweled, of golden leather and semiprecious stones—will be made for you by a jeweler and given you. A beautiful blue curtain and a blue carpet will be the setting, along with a special brass frame set with blue stones. It, too, will belong to you. In addition, you will get five hundred francs. This will be your debut as a professional dancer."

"But what happened? It's fantastic." I sat down, hugging my shabby ballet bag.

"It all happened because you said *no*." Mother chuckled

delightedly. "The poor woman is very wealthy. She has a great deal of money and is used to paying for anything she wants, at least ten times what it is worth. She's married to an Italian and enjoys giving parties. She came to call on me when that Mr. Brown-Smith told her you had refused to dance. She's a good-hearted soul and determined to have you. She's going to help that 'pretty little thing,' meaning you, even if it does cost a mint to do it."

"I never heard of such a thing," I said. "A woman spending all that money."

"She's spending it to get what she wants," Mother answered. "You, who hate Oriental dancing, will not only dance an Oriental dance, but your body and face will be painted blue and you'll have blue hair——"

"I won't dye my hair!"

"Of course not, it'll be a wig," she soothed me. "Really, Regina, this ball is unbelievable. Some famous artist has conceived the idea, and she is mounting it in her grand ballroom. Everyone who performs will be given the costumes and the settings he appears in."

"What does she use for money?" I asked.

Mother answered, "Oil wells!"

"Do you really want me to do it? Dance that loathesome Oriental stuff?"

"Do as you please," Mother answered. "But if you want to be seen, I'd say this was the chance of a lifetime, even if you had nine lives."

Her reasoning was too sound to dispute. I took some lessons and found Oriental dancing to be a fascinating type of religious ceremony. The exquisite movement of body, head, hands, and eyes which I was taught was centuries old. Soon I realized that Kathakali dancing was not a matter of wiggles and undulations at all; rather, was it the lifework of serious, consecrated artists.

I was busy and happy. Each morning I had a lesson with Mme. Stichel. Almost every afternoon I took class with M. Staats. Sometimes I had a fitting. Whenever possible, a lesson in Oriental dancing was sandwiched in. Usually around five-thirty Mother and I had a high tea of cold meat, brioches, delicate and hot from the patisserie around the corner, and scorching, heartening tea. It was a filling and inexpensive meal. Occasionally I posed for a famous artist, but on those days I would be exhausted when I arrived home at nine or ten o'clock. However, a hot bath and a poached egg on toast would give me strength to face whatever late dancing engagement I might have, which was always well after midnight.

Mme. Rienzini's ball proved a high light in my career. I was announced as *La Petite Danseuse Américaine Vouée au Bleu*. My name was changed to Nila Devi, meaning the Blue Goddess in Sanskrit, or so I was told. My dance was called *L'Idole Turquoise*, and opened with me standing in a replica of the golden frame of the god Siva in the Musée Guimet. That particular little statue in its golden circle has given rise to many stage settings. I lay no claim to being the first to use it. The jeweled frame which was made for me was solid brass and contained some very handsome theatrical stones. I posed immobile for nearly three minutes, then descended to the gasps of the audience and danced. Many dancers must have posed using the god Siva as a model long before I did, and many more will use him in the years to come.

Now I know that *L'Idole Turquoise*, which I thought was an original idea of Mr. Brown-Smith's for me, was nothing more than a musical comedy rehash of Nijinsky's *Le Dieu Bleu*. A pity indeed that I was too self-centered to realize that such a ballet was in the Diaghileff repertoire; but if I had, I doubtless would not have had any career at all. I would have known at once that I was a mere and palpable imitation of the real thing. Certainly ignorance was bliss. In my case it would indeed have been folly to be wise.

Fittings for my unbelievably beautiful costume for *L'Idole Turquoise* were a nightmare. A jeweled costume is fitted by a craftsman with a pair of pliers, which means he had to undo little rings of metal and pinch them together again to make the jeweled scrolls fit. Most of the time he pinched me as well as the little metal rings.

My blue wig was fitted, various shades of blue paste were tried out on a model's skin for me to see, and finally a color was decided upon. Because making up my whole body was irksome and I had so little time, full make-up was not applied till the night itself.

The ball was a blaze of color, but the entertainment of which I was one small part was Scheherazade's *One Thousand and One Nights* all crammed into a single evening. About 4:00 A.M., when the performance was over and the applause had died away, a footman came to invite all of us performers to come mingle with Madame's guests.

This was the big moment for us. As we filed from the specially built stage in her grand ballroom, we had to pass the dias on which Madame Rienzini stood wrapped in cloth of gold. Torrents of glittering diamonds cascaded down her front. She wore a spiky jeweled tiara on her head. A purple cloak lined with ermine hung from her shoulders. One at a time with a cordial smile and a few words of praise she handed each of us a crested envelope containing our wages and the bills of sale for our scenery and costumes. The women curtsied low while the men bent almost double to kiss her hand. It was all excessively, blatantly *nouveau riche,* but Madame Rienzini was so happy in her role of Lady Bountiful that we entertainers would have been ingrates if we had not accepted her gifts in the spirit in which she gave them.

Back home, exhausted but filled with joy over my gifts and

the cash bonus of $125, Mother and I envisaged a life of ease and luxury. I took off my wig and cold-creamed my blue face. It looked shinier and bluer than ever. The make-up cloth remained pristine white. I rubbed, I scrubbed, I tried hot water and soap. Mother used alcohol and toilet water. The color remained.

"You're dyed blue!" Mother gasped. "Oh, dear. Will it ever fade? What will we do? You can't go round Paris *that* color."

"Not vowed to blue," I exclaimed hysterically, bursting into tears, "but dyed, dyed to blue. Maybe it'll never come off and I'll be buried as a blue goddess." Then I added, "You know, I itch."

"Oh, no!" Mother grabbed for the phone. "We'll call a doctor. I expect you're poisoned."

The doctor arrived, ordered a soothing lotion, and informed us that if I were poisoned, there was nothing *he* could do about it. If we were such fools as to cover the body with an unknown substance, we would have to take the consequences. He took the blue paste with him to have analyzed, suggested I go to bed, put a pill on my tongue, handed me a glass of water, and said he would go home to breakfast, a new day had begun.

It had indeed. I slept fitfully through it. Word came that the mixture was nontoxic. The itching had ceased. The doctor ordered a warm bath every three hours, complete bed rest, and plenty of cool drinks. "Time," he assured us, "is of the essence."

Very, very slowly the color faded. Five days later I was a nice robin's-egg blue. It took all of two weeks before I paled to an odd grayish-white which would permit me to pass unnoticed on the street.

"Never again," Mother said. "One lives and learns."

chapter 15:   *Audition at the Folies Bergère*

"Did you say I was ill of some mysterious disease?" I asked
Mother the first day I went downstairs. We were on the
ascenseur, drifting downward slowly and jerkily. Only a
French elevator can give that odd sense of freedom from
gravity, as if at any moment it might, if it chose, go off sideways and float away like a balloon.

"I told them the truth, that you had the blues, quite literally, that not only did you feel blue but you were blue."

"Oh, Mother. They'll think I'm a freak."

"You were," Mother said. "It gave me a turn to look at
you. I quite shivered every time for fear you'd never be
white again. Brown or tan or yellow would have been all
right, but a bright-blue child is something else again. Anyway, your fingernails and around your eyes and ears are still
pretty blue. We couldn't deny it, so why bother?"

I was an interesting phenomenon for a few days, but interest soon vanished with the news of a booking at the Coliseum. Several acts from Madame Rienzini's party had appeared. Now I could, if I chose, dance there for a week. I would get $100, or 500 francs. The old cliché that I would be seen by many theatrical producers and agents was worked to death. The only drawback was their insistence that I must be blue.

"No," we said over and over again. "White with a blue wig, with a blue spotlight."

"Blue all over." The management was adamant. "The person *bleu*."

"We will ask the doctor if a lotion can be made which will wash off," Mother said. "If one can be, she will appear. If one cannot, she won't."

The doctor bristled, stated he was a serious medical man and had no time to play games with crazy Americans who wished to change the color of their skins. Finally he agreed, on learning that I would be paid 500 francs, for one franc in 1913 was worth twenty cents in American money.

"*Voyons!*" he shouted. "Why did you not say so before? *Enfin,* if so much money is involved, we will indeed color the young lady like a rainbow."

For 25 francs he made a lotion that was applied with absorbent cotton and washed off completely with soap and water. It was, I suspect, the usual calamine lotion for mosquito bites, tinted blue instead of pink. At any rate it worked.

I signed my contract, I danced, I was applauded politely. I created not a ripple theatrically. After each performance I stepped into a washtub of hot water laboriously brought to my dressing room in small jugs. Mother scrubbed and I scrubbed, and I emerged pink and white instead of Copenhagen blue.

161

The Coliseum offered to extend my contract.

"No, thank you," Mother said. "I didn't come to Paris to be a washerwoman. All I do day and night is scrub that child from head to foot. It's idiotic and undignified. I have always dealt in paints, but I rebel at this continued painting of my daughter's body."

We did not sign, and the only token of my week's appearance at the Coliseum was an offer to tour the provinces at 350 francs a week, not worthy of our consideration. Traveling expenses, expressing my drapes and props, and living in small hotels would certainly cost more than that small sum.

Back in classes, I found myself singled out for attention. I had made a debut. The notices, though small, were uniformly good. My friends considered me very successful. I didn't feel successful at all. I began to wonder what in the world I did want. I was in demand for teas and soirees. Now that I was "professional," I was being paid anywhere from $25 to $50 a performance. My posing was making me well known in the art world and Madame Paquin had met me and decided to make me some frocks. All I had to do to repay her was to say that she had made them, if anyone inquired, and quote the price.

I came back from class early one day with a splitting headache. I was dizzy and out of sorts.

"You should wear a hat, not a beret," Mother said. "You're sunburned."

"In March! How silly."

"You are being very rude and edgy lately," Mother said. "Don't you feel well?"

"Yes . . . no. I don't know. My head aches and I've strained a dozen muscles. I feel awful, and I'm supposed to audition for M. Berenger at the Folies Bergère tomorrow. It's really set. Just imagine. Six of us from M. Staats's class have been selected to try out.

"But if you're ill——"

"I can't be ill," I snapped. "I won't be. I don't want any supper. I'm going to bed."

Mother said something about success not having improved me any, and in my heart I agreed with her. I could have added that I wasn't happy about it either. Being disagreeable brought me no pleasure or comfort. I merely felt worse.

I took a couple of headache pills at midnight and slept fitfully. At nine o'clock Mother was dressed to go out. I was tempted to tell her I felt awful and to ask her to please call the doctor, but instead I growled I wanted to sleep longer and please go away. No, I didn't want the curtains up or a cup of tea! Hadn't I said I wanted to sleep? She set the alarm for ten, and I dozed.

When I finally heard the alarm and got out of bed, my head spun and the furniture danced. I showered, powdered hastily, making faces at myself in the wavy mirror. It certainly made me look monstrously ugly. My face seemed awfully pink and puffy, but I shrugged it off. After all, most bathroom mirrors made one look like a hag. I dressed dreamily and wavered downstairs. There were no taxis in sight, so I stepped into a horse-drawn cab. The poor horse slipped and slithered on the freshly washed street, and I shook and shivered in sympathy, but the trip to the Folies Bergère was a short one, and happily I arrived without accident.

To actually enter the theater of my dreams by the stage door gave me a tremendous sense of elation. I was dressed for my audition and merely peeled off my dress and put on my toe slippers. There were only six of us backstage. The theater was full of morning quiet. I began to practice as the others were doing stretching and limbering exercises.

"A little powder?" One girl offered me a puff. "You return from exposure to the sun at the Côte d'Azur?"

"No," I said. "Do I look sunburned?"

"But, yes, you are definitely quite badly burned." She shrugged. "You are perhaps susceptible to the sun's rays."

"Not at all." I shook my head.

"You are not well?" another girl asked. "You would like to sniff camphor?"

"I am perfectly well," I snapped. "Stop trying to get me to quit this audition. All you want is to have less competition. I'm perfectly well and I'm going to dance."

"*Alors*, what rudeness! It is the American way. All Americans are rude."

"*Mesdemoiselles*." M. Berenger appeared. We lined up and were arranged according to height. A small blonde danced first.

"The corps," M. Berenger said. "Perhaps a small solo."

A redhead danced next. "The corps—a solo." He smiled.

I danced. His, "No, *allons!*" was explosive. "*Pas possible. Qu 'est-ce qu'elle fait?*" he demanded of no one in particular. I hurried off stage not paying any attention to what was going on there. I dressed, impatiently skipping buttons which wouldn't button. My head ached so I could hardly see. There seemed to be a battering ram behind my eyes.

Ready to leave, I came face to face with M. Berenger at the stage door. "I'm sorry you didn't like my dancing," I said. "I do so want to dance here at the Folies. It's been my ambition to dance here ever since I began to study. I know I'm not a classic ballerina, I don't aspire to Opera ballet, but I'd give anything in the world to be in one of your lovely ballets."

"Sorry," he said briefly, "*pas de possibilité*. I don't like your dancing at all. You might as well make up your mind that you will never dance here at my theater. Please do not waste your time or mine by ever auditioning again for me. You are clumsy and you are also very peculiar to look at, especially the face. You would not do at all for the Folies."

I stumbled onto the sidewalk. My head was spinning. I

had never known such an absolutely complete turn-down. Never before had anyone been so outspoken. "Clumsy" and "very peculiar to look at." It was the end of my dream of the capitulation of Paris to my charms. The Folies put on the loveliest ballets outside the real Opera ballet groups, and if the Folies was closed to me, as it certainly was, just where would I dance? I didn't know. My head ached, I itched all over, I felt miserable, and all that I'd accomplished up to now seemed to be for naught. It was so odd. Never before had anyone seemed to think I was very peculiar to look at. I knew I wasn't beautiful, but peculiar! Especially the face! How dreadful!

I hailed a cab. A man stopped and assisted me in. I had difficulty with the steps and fell into the seat. I mumbled my address. At the hotel I gave the driver my pocketbook, for even after it was open, I couldn't seem to see the money. The *ascenseur* door seemed very heavy, but I got in and out under my own power. I was too exhausted, however, to climb the last flight of stairs. I sat for a while, crying quietly, and then crawled up them. Arriving on my hands and knees in our sitting room, I was quite unprepared for Mother's screams. They seemed so unreasonable that I forgot about them and closed my eyes, lying quietly on the floor, thankful to be home, even if I was home to a mother who raised her hands in horror at the sight of me and shrieked, "Oh, no! Not again! Who has painted you red?"

Some time later I opened my eyes to find myself in bed with a starched angel wearing a flaring white coif sitting beside me. She was staring at me with big blue anxious eyes, trying to slip a bit of ice held in a cloth between my lips.

"Am I dreadfully sick?" I asked weakly, licking at it with my tongue. "Please tell me. Where is my mother? What is the matter with me?" I tried to rise in bed, but she laid me back gently.

"Have no fear," she told me. "You have a childish sickness called the black measles. It strikes very suddenly. The skin becomes very dark red and angry. There is a high fever. It will last at most two weeks. You have been quite ill for several days. The spots are still very bad. You will please sleep now." She gave me some medicine. "The doctor has attended you most faithfully," she added. "Your color now is red, not black. As for your *maman*, she had such fear that you would die that she did not sleep an instant till your fever went down early this morning."

At lunchtime Mother came in to me. She relieved the nurse and spooned cold custard into my mouth.

"Sometime," she said, "we may think this all very funny, but I don't believe I will ever get such a shock again as I did when you came crawling into that room on all fours. You were absolutely mahogany color, and sort of spotty into the bargain. Then you passed out cold. I thought you'd been painted up for another role. When I found you were ill, I nearly went crazy."

"M. Berenger said I looked peculiar." I spoke weakly. "Mother, do you suppose I was that awful color when I danced? I know I felt funny and dizzy and I stumbled a couple of times. The girls thought I was sunburned."

"You very likely looked like a slice of rare beef steak," Mother said decisively. "I do not believe anyone could get the color you were all of a sudden. How did you ever have sense enough to take a cab?"

"I don't know," I admitted. "Someone put me in. I know I just gave the driver my purse when I got here. I couldn't see the money."

"I wondered what had happened," Mother said. "Your driver thought you were drunk. There was a note inside your purse which said, 'Have taken 4 francs. *Pauvre petite. C'est vraiment dommage.*' At first I couldn't understand why he

166

said that it was a terrible shame, then I realized he thought you'd been drinking. You poor child. What an experience."

I nodded. "But it doesn't matter so much now," I told her. "You see, if I was peculiar-looking because I had the black measles . . . What are they anyway?" I interrupted myself to ask.

"A very severe form of regular measles; so much blood is released under the skin that it looks quite black. The doctor explained it to me. He said you had a bad case."

"I see," I said. "Do you suppose my dancing was peculiar because I was sick? If so, then it wouldn't be me or my dancing that M. Berenger turned down, but a girl with black measles who looked horrible and danced dreadfully."

"No doubt, no doubt," Mother said, and turned to explain to the nurse that talking would never give me a relapse. "She'll be better for it," Mother assured her. "Really, she will be, you'll see."

Getting well took weeks, and even then I was wobbly on my legs. It was May before I was able to dance again, to take up my posing and fittings and to appear at the soirees when I was asked. I found the nicest thing about having been ill was the concern my friends exhibited by sending fruit, flowers, and their cars to take us to drive.

"A little fresh air would do marvels," they urged, and a little fresh air, or a whole lot taken in a Daimler or a Panhard town car, suited us perfectly. Where before we had taken buses or dirty, noisy trams, we now were wafted endless miles through glorious countryside. We enjoyed every moment, and soon became as confirmed sight-seers as we ever had been in London. Chauffeurs and footmen, we soon found out, did not care whether they drove in the park or to the museums, and a substantial tip endeared us more to them than any pretense that we were above the scenic wonders they showed us. We had begun to know Paris and its environs well. We had seen Versailles often, once at night with colored lights playing on the shivering, gleaming fountains. It was the most breath-taking sight we had ever seen, and made us realize how paltry any theatrical setting could ever be.

Friends from the United States and England kept arriving, and Mother and I were hard put to it to do the honors. Even my own Uncle Ferd found it difficult to believe that classes, posing, and fittings kept me busy the whole day through, and that nearly every night I was dancing and being paid for it at some private gathering.

Preparing to go to the bank one day, Mother looked up from balancing our checkbook.

"Would you mind if I showed Ferd these checks?" she asked. "He just looks so skeptically at me when I say Daddy doesn't send us any money. I know he doesn't believe a word of it when I say you send it to him, and that you've already sent back over a thousand dollars."

"You ought to add that Father is banking it for me. Does Ferd know Daddy is all paid up and making money again?"

"I'm sure he does," Mother said. "He had dinner with your father and Aunt Barb a couple of weeks ago. He says they are opening the house in June. He said your father was talking of buying a car. He says horses are obsolete."

"Horses obsolete! I can't believe Father said that! Certainly Starlight isn't. I just can't imagine Father driving a car, can you?"

"No," Mother said, "but perhaps you will someday."

At dinner that night Uncle Ferd was so polite and respectful, he didn't seem like my uncle at all. He treated me like a grownup of whom he was slightly in awe.

"He was so impressed by that checkbook," Mother said afterward. "He kept saying, 'You were right, Gene, she did have talent. It's paying off. She's a smart girl.' "

Mrs. Mond passed through Paris and sent her maid to see

us with little gifts and a message of congratulation. Lady Violet came to call, and showed more surprise at my excellent French accent than she did at my drawing-room success, which she seemed to take for granted.

By June first, most of the casting for the summer shows was finished. Outside of my lessons and my after-midnight engagements I was posing for Raphael Kirchner. I found sitting for a portrait far more tiring than dance poses, where I could move freely when I chose. Actually, movement often gave the artists new perspective on his line, whereas any change of expression disturbed a portrait painter.

June is one of the loveliest months anywhere in the world; it is especially lovely in Paris, but it meant nothing to me. I grew more and more worried as the days passed. I was making quite a good deal of money, we were having a good time, but both my mother and I were restless and unsure. I hadn't gone to London to study dancing merely to become an entertainer at small fashionable parties or great glamorous soirees. We both knew that a great deal of my present success was due to my novelty. In six months a long-legged Swede or a gamin-type Hungarian dancer would come along to charm fickle audiences and take my place. I was the center of attraction now, but we both knew there was no certainty as to how long I would remain fortune's favorite.

On June fifth Mother said, "What say we find out about a Cook's tour to Austria-Hungary? There won't be much doing here in the summer, and we've plenty of money for a nice holiday."

"All right," I agreed. "I'd like to travel, but let's go second class. I'd like just to be a tourist again. I'll wear old clothes and be your little girl."

Mother laughed, and in her laugh was a certain sharpness.

"I'm sorry," she said, "but I'd just like to see your face the first time some unfortunate gentleman assumed you were a schoolgirl from the United States. Anyway, your French would give you away. You give orders like a *grande dame*."

"I don't believe a word of it," I said pettishly. "I'm the same as I ever was."

"No, you're not, dear." Mother said cheerfully. "You've survived some very hard battles for success; you've danced for the elite of Paris for five months, and you show it. You're a charming, poised, hard-boiled young woman. You're not the little innocent, unsophisticated baby that arrived in Paris. You've done a lot of growing up, and if I say it as shouldn't, you've done a very nice job of it. I'm proud of you."

"Why, Mother," I gasped. "How can you be? Here I am with thousands of lessons behind me and not a job in sight, to say nothing of having been turned down good and hard at the only theater I really want to dance in."

"So it still rankles that M. Berenger said *never?*" Mother asked. "Just forget it. There are other and better theaters. You'll succeed yet, just as you want to succeed."

"Sez you!" I answered bleakly.

"Well, I'm off," she told me and shut the door. I shrugged and went out on the roof into the sunshine. It was warm and sunny. Paris glittered as it lay spread out before me. I could see the Basilica of Sacré-Coeur high on the hills of Montmartre. The sky was blue, the Tuileries were green, the bulk of the Paris Opera was brown stone, and I could see the green-gray copper roof. I was restless and discontented. I knew I had accomplished a great deal more than I'd ever really expected to accomplish, and that what I wanted, I couldn't possibly have. When a man says *never*, in the tone of voice M. Berenger had used, he didn't mean *maybe*.

The phone rang. I was of half a mind not to answer, but its insistent rasping buzz finally brought me inside.

"*Allo,*" I snapped. "*Allo. Oui, c'est moi.* What do you wish?"

chapter 16:   *Second Chance*

THE MAN on the other end of the wire was insistent and obstinate.

"*Mademoiselle*," he pleaded. "I have seen you dance. Be kind enough to do me this favor. Go to this tiny *boîte* off the Champs-Elysées at nine o'clock. A loge is reserved for you. Dress please, in your very best. I assure you that this will be to your advantage."

"To my advantage to do you the favor of going to a small theater?" I asked. "Who are you? This doesn't make sense."

"All in due time," he purred. "At the moment there is nothing more to say. You promise me? You will go? Please, I beg of you."

"Oh, well," I said, weakening suddenly. "I promise. Why not? I am going on a vacation tomorrow or the next day. It makes no difference to me what I do tonight, but it seems to make a great difference to you."

"And to you also, *petite*," the words were whispered. Then a click, and the connection was broken.

"We have a date," I told Mother when she returned, her hands full of Cook's tour leaflets. "Tonight we are to go to a small theater, dressed in our very best. A loge is reserved for us."

"Who with?" Mother asked idly.

"An unknown with a voice like silk velvet. Someone who insists that this favor to him will be of advantage to me."

"And he isn't meeting you there?"

"He didn't say," I answered. "He just hung up."

"Perhaps it is a joke. Perhaps there will be no loge, and we will be all dressed up and have nowhere to go."

"That is quite possible," I agreed, "but if we are stood up, we will go to some other theater and sit down, even if we have to pay to see the show. If we pay," I said shortly, "we can at least go to something we want to see. *Le Malade Imaginaire* is at the Comédie Française. That might be fun."

Mother agreed. She had brought home delicious *croissants*, cold ham, potato salad, and a cherry tart. We ate, sitting out on the roof, at a rather wobbly table with a blue-checked cloth.

"This is fun," I said. "I'd rather stay here than go to any little *boîte*."

"Nevertheless, we're going," Mother said, picking up some of the empty dishes. "I want to find out if we've been hoaxed, and if so, we must allow enough time to get to the Comédie Française."

"Oh, very well." Languidly I trailed after her with the rest of the dishes, folded the cloth, and carried the rickety table into the bedroom.

"What'll I wear?" I demanded from the closet.

"Your sapphire-blue velvet suit, pearls, and the tight little pearl cap," Mother answered. "I'll wear my black taffeta and feather boa."

The sapphire velvet suit made by Paquin was lovely, soft, lustrous, gloriously rich in shimmering folds. I was proudest, though, of the sandal shoes in blue suede which matched exactly. I pulled on white doeskin gloves, then hurried back from the elevator to get the turquoise-and-brilliant bracelet.

"Why not the sapphire-and-pearl pin?" Mother asked. "That bracelet doesn't match at all."

"I think it is a lucky bracelet," I said softly. "It was Mrs. Mond's favorite bit of jewelry. It's mine, too."

"I hope it does bring you luck," Mother said, smiling. "But how much more you are entitled to, I don't know. Do you realize how lucky you are right now? You're exquisitely dressed by the best *couturière* in Paris at no expense, you are wearing lovely, if not real, jewelry, you are making several hundred dollars a week, you have your health, and you are only seventeen years old."

"I know," I admitted. I was trying to explain to the taxi driver where we wished to go.

He demurred. I argued. He raised his hands and waved them. "Crazy Americans," he said, and shrugged.

"What was the matter with him?"

"I don't know for sure," I answered. "It seems he does not feel that the little *boîte* we're headed for is the right little *boîte* for ladies."

"Maybe it isn't!" Mother took a firmer hold on her umbrella. "Maybe we'll be murdered or shot."

"More likely we'll be propositioned," I said, giggling. "Don't you dare say *yes* to anything unless I say it first, do you understand?"

Mother nodded. She knew her penchant for saying *yes*

173

was dangerous. *"Oui, oui,"* she would say, smiling, and those *yeses* had more than once got her into trouble. We both remembered one day when we were walking along the Champs-Elysées, enjoying a stroll after our early supper. A handsome gentleman, with neatly trimmed Vandyke beard, caped overcoat, and tall hat accosted us. He bowed low over Mother's hand and kissed it.

He spoke very rapid Gatling gun French.

"Non, Monsieur," I said. "Absolutely no!"

"Mais oui," Mother contradicted me. *"Mais certainement.* It will give us great pleasure."

"Alors!" He looked at me. "Why do you say *no?* The *maman* says *yes."*

"Maman est idiote," I answered rudely, and taking her arm, hauled her away.

"Now is that nice?" she asked. "Why shouldn't the nice gentleman walk with us and give us a Dubonnet? Who was he, anyway?"

"That's what I'd like to know," I said, half laughing. "Mother, you're a precious fool. The 'gentleman' took us for light ladies and wanted our company for no good purpose!"

"What!" Mother turned toward our would-be escort, who was still at our heels, and glowered at him, waving her umbrella menacingly. He turned and fled, no doubt in his mind as to what she meant.

"You must be very careful about saying *yes* here in Paris," I continued as the cab braked to a stop. "It's different than in London."

"Regina," Mother said blandly. "You can stop lecturing me. I really know the facts of life."

We paid the chauffeur, who cast dark looks at the gaily lighted entrance. He didn't drive off, though, until he saw us pick up tickets at the box-office window and vanish inside.

It was a lovely little theater, holding at most two hundred people. The stage was small and intimate, the curtains, rose-colored, as was the seat upholstery. The tiny auditorium was exquisitely lighted by flattering pink-shaded crystal chandeliers.

A man in evening dress was on stage, smirking and singing naughty songs. I couldn't make out the joke, though I could understand a word or two here and there. Parisian argot is a language in itself, and only experience broad and varied can make it intelligible.

We sat in our little loge and began to enjoy the show when two French soldiers appeared and launched on a comic routine. No one came near us, and we decided the manager had merely wished to dress the boxes well, for the six loges were all occupied by extremely attractive young women. About eleven o'clock an envelope was passed to me by a page in scarlet and gold. The note said simply that Monsieur Paul Franck was casting for two new ballets and would like to see me in his office. I whispered the good news to Mother and hurried off.

M. Franck kissed my hand and informed me in exquisite French that I was a ravishingly beautiful creature. With these amenities out of the way he became extremely businesslike, and explained that because the star of his new revue had defaulted, he was a producer with a show about to open —and no star.

"It seems," he said bitterly, "that Madame prefers to amuse herself on the Riviera rather than keep her contract to act, sing, and dance in my revue. And yet, *Mademoiselle,* my show is scheduled to open in ten days." He ruffled his thick hair with exquisitely manicured fingers, shrugged his well-tailored shoulders, and bugged his brown eyes at me. I looked as sympathetic as I could in the face of a possible job.

"Now," he continued, "I have acquired a dramatic actress and a singing star, but I still need a young and lovely dancer. That is why the open audition. Very quickly, we must find a dark horse on which to bet our money, and it cannot be too great a sum. I hope you will agree to audition. I think you have possibilities."

These words sounded musically in my ears, and I assured him that I would be at the Étoile Palace the following day at 9:00 A.M.

Actually, it was a few minutes before nine the next morning when I entered the Étoile Palace, in which the auditions would be held. I felt very much at home in this cool, dim theater, for it was here that Madame Stichel held her classes when it was free. Madame believed that a dancer who was to dance on stage should practice on stage; therefore she always hired an empty theater to use as her classroom. Thanks to her foresight, I had already become accustomed to the limited space between the wings as well as to the slanted stage. I was also aware that the footlights were an arbitrary dividing line which a pirouetting dancer must not ignore. Indeed, I had learned by experience that if I didn't stop before reaching them, I would fall into the orchestra pit.

There were about a hundred and fifty girls present at the audition, grouped in various spots in the auditorium. Some were knitting, others, reading and gossiping. All were well back from the third row, where Monsieur Franck and his colleagues were sitting.

Stage lights came on, and a man entered from the wings.

"Stand back and be counted," he shouted. "All you who dance. Not the *mamans* nor the gentleman attendants." A

176

ripple of laughter passed over the room as a flood of girls dashed down the aisles.

"One twenty-nine, one thirty," he counted carefully, and as each girl was counted, she sat down. "One hundred and seventy-three." He lifted a tall hat. "Into this these will go," he picked up pile after pile of square cardboards from a small table and dropped them into the hat. "Exactly one hundred and seventy-three numbers. Get in line please, *mesdemoiselles*. You will draw your audition number as you pass me by. Quickly now. You understand, one person only is to be chosen. The choice is final. No complaints, no recriminations. The decision is up to the judges. *Allons y*."

We filed by him rapidly. Occasionally a girl held up the line searching, searching, but he would hurry her on, saying one could not change one's luck, it was bad luck to try.

I was overjoyed to find that I had drawn number twenty-four. At least with such a low number I might have a chance to try out for the role.

M. Franck then went on stage.

"This audition is an attempt to discover new dancing talent, an *originale*, I might say. All of you are doubtless excellent dancers. Not to be taken is not to be construed as an insult. We do not know what we are looking for, but we are sure we will know it when we see it. There are two scenes. A gypsy dance, *La Feria*, and a lovely lyric dance called *Le Bain de Phryné*. *Décor* and music are set. The dancer must fit herself to them. The music will be played, you will dance. There is no formula for the audition. That is all. I thank you."

The theater buzzed with comment, mostly unfavorable. How could one go on stage and dance, just like that? What a crazy way to audition people!

"Seat yourselves in the order of your coming on stage,"

a man in shirt sleeves ordered. "Let's get this over with. *Numéro un.*" We milled about in the aisles, those of us with low numbers pressing forward. A tall girl beside me was complaining of the heat.

"It is unbearable," she told me, crowding close. "I feel quite faint."

"I don't think it's so hot." I edged forward, trying to pass her. She elbowed me rudely, swayed, and fell heavily against me. As I stretched out my hands to break her fall, my own number fell to the ground. She groaned, moved slightly, and sat up, weaving a little dizzily. She picked up my card and handed it back to me.

"Your *numéro,*" she told me. "You should be more careful. Someone please give me a hand."

A dozen hands were offered. She was dusted off, patted, and led to a seat in the fifth row of the orchestra. I pushed forward and sat down in the sixth row, clutching my precious number twenty-four in my hand. I watched, fascinated, as the girls danced and were dismissed. Some were waved off after a few steps. Number Thirteen was kept dancing for some time, but the judges apparently disagreed, for she eventually was dismissed. When Number Seventeen disappeared, I began to feel very nervous. I smoothed out my ticket. The number on it smote me in the face. It was not twenty-four, but one hundred and three. How had this happened? How could it have happened? I had held it in my hand. . . .

But no. The girl who fainted had knocked it from my hand. She had picked it up from the floor and given it back to me. Or so I had thought. Instead, she must have switched the numbers. Surely I had hers and she, mine. But was it deliberate? If so, her faint had been but a bit of play-acting. I bent forward and touched her shoulder.

"What is your number, Miss?"

"And what is that to you?" She snapped. "It is not your affair, Mees Amerika, but I will tell you. My *numéro* is twenty-four."

"I see." I wondered what would happen if I rose and said she had stolen my number. I could imagine the laughter, the amused glances at my charge. "Crazy American" would be the verdict. Oh, how I hoped she would fail! I willed her to fall down flat, to break an ankle, to tear a ligament. Nothing of the sort happened. She danced very well and was detained in conversation by the judges, but eventually she, too, left the stage and Number Twenty-five was called.

There was a break for lunch, and later, for afternoon coffee and hot brioches. Number Eighty-seven was waved off without even being permitted to start.

"Too big," she was told. "Too big. The chorus is only five-two."

When Number One Hundred was called, we were surprised; then we realized that several girls who had numbers in the nineties had left without waiting to be called. It wasn't so very unreasonable, as a girl beside me muttered. "What would they? Perfection in face and form they have had often, and all dance well."

"You speak the truth," I answered. Suddenly she moved forward. She was Number One Hundred and Two. I held my breath while she danced. A judge motioned her to come over to him. He wrote something on his card and gave it to her. Then she went away. I jumped when my number was called and hurried on stage. I realized now I should have been limbering up, not just sitting.

The music for *La Feria,* the gypsy dance, sounded in my ears. I had heard it over and over. Unconsciously I had fitted my woodland mymph dance steps to it. I forgot I was auditioning. I just danced.

The silence at the end was absolute.

"*Alors, Le Bain de Phryné*," M. Franck snapped. "What are we waiting for?"

Here I was in my element. Lyric plastic dancing, the fore-runner of modern dance. Now I didn't care whether I was taken or not. The judges of my dancing seemed instead to represent the judges before whom Phryne was dancing. She had to prove her innocence by the purity of her dancing. This innocence of evil was something I knew all about. I felt as if I were Phryne in body and spirit. I danced my heart out, and prostrated myself before my judges on the last notes.

Now I was being helped up. Such a gabbling was in my ears, I was dazed and uncomprehending.

"Come with me, my little one, my dove," M. Franck pleaded. "Come sign the contract."

"You mean I am chosen? That I will be in your revue?" He nodded. "But yes, *Mademoiselle*. Of a certainty. Please come this way." I followed docilely, not believing that I had heard aright or that this could be really happening to me. I had dreamed of it, of course, but that it should actually be taking place did not seem possible.

I signed my name wherever I was told to and was quite unprepared for the shocked looks and violent scoldings which ensued when I agreed that though I did not "have a great age, I already had seventeen years!"

It took some time for me to understand that legally seventeen years were too few to sign a contract and that therefore my *maman* would have to sign, too.

"I will telephone my *maman*," I said as soon as I understood him. "Remain *tranquille*. She will come at once and sign."

"*Attends, un moment.*" The ballet master and *régisseur* spoke at the same instant. "Measurements for costume first of all." He waved at a little man standing nearby, nervously running a long yellow tape measure through his hands. "Then we must go over the steps and set them."

"You will telephone the *maman* in one little moment," M. Franck assured me over and over again. But each time I was caught up and pushed this way and that. As I was measured for costumes, I saw the steps I had done being tried out in a very outsize way by the ballet master. "So?" he would ask. "*Ça te plaît?*" If I remembered them at all, I would nod vaguely; if I didn't, I would shrug, secure only in the fact that once I was free of these deftly entangling hands measuring me so carefully, I would once again recapture the steps, or even better ones, from the sheer joy of dancing.

Everyone had left the auditorium except for two girls, my best friends at the Leo Staats School. They came down during a pause in my measuring and congratulated me.

"Ha," M. Franck said. "This is a pretty gesture. You are nice girls. Have you auditioned?" They shook their heads. "Come in tomorrow, if you wish, and do so," he said grandly. "There is always room in the corps for two more *petites si gentilles*—if they can dance," he added menacingly.

They fell on me with cries of joy. "We'll see you tomorrow," they chattered. "What did we tell you? You bring us luck," and they pinched me very hard indeed to prove it. There is no better way, at least in Europe, to make sure that luck will hold than by pinching the lucky one until she squeals, be she pig or person.

My squeals reminded everyone of work to be done.

"No, no." I could *not* telephone as of this moment. I must get to work. There was plenty of time to telephone. "*Attends, petite.* Did it go like this or like that?"

The music played. M. Franck watched fondly. Time passed. I forgot *maman*, the telephone, everything in the excitement of rehearsal.

It was hours later when a commotion in the auditorium caught our attention.

"*Qu'est-ce que c'est?*" the ballet master asked. "What is this? *Pourquoi* police?"

As he spoke, I recognized my mother between two excited gendarmes, still arguing with a frantic stage doorman.

"Mother! What happened? Are you arrested?" I knelt by the footlights in my anxiety.

"Certainly not!" Mother's cheeks were very red, her Queen Mary toque slightly askew. "What are you doing up on that stage? Do you realize what time it is, young lady? It is one o'clock in the morning, and I have been trying to get into this theater since nine o'clock to find out if you were here. All I was told was, '*Pas possible.* All are gone. Only principals remain.' I was sure you had been taken ill or lured into white slavery, so I went to the police. Just what is going on?"

"I won the audition, Mama," I said. "I am rehearsing. I wanted to phone you, but they wouldn't let me stop rehearsing, and then I forgot all about it. I've been measured for costumes. Madame Paquin is going to make them for me. The show opens in ten days."

All this time M. Franck was soothing the gendarmes. Soon, armed with passes for themselves and wives, they pattered off, capes flying, first bowing politely to me and to Mama. Now M. Franck bent over Mother's hand and kissed it. He begged that she sign the contract. Mother balked! "We should have a lawyer see this," she told me. "Heaven knows what we're signing this way, all this fine print in a foreign language."

"It doesn't matter!" I shouted. "It's just a regular contract. It says I'm going to dance in Monsieur Franck's revue. Please, please don't make a fuss, Mother. Just sign!"

When she finally gave in, neither of us knew that I had

182

signed a contract as *Danseuse Étoile* at 500 francs a week, which, in 1913, meant one hundred prewar dollars and was a very good salary indeed for a beginner.

"You will take *La Petite* home?" M. Franck asked Mother later on. "If so, we will call the rehearsal off; she must be *très fatiguée*." He turned to me. "Tomorrow rehearsal is at nine o'clock. You will have a fitting in the afternoon, at Madame Paquin's. Then we will rehearse again. *Çe te plaît?* You will arrive promptly?"

"Oh, yes!" I assured him. "I will be here on the very dot of nine. Maybe before."

"Not here!" M. Franck put up his hand. "We rehearse where we will play. You will please to come to the Folies Bergère, on the Boulevard des Italiens. The house is not mine, of course," he explained, "but I have rented it from Monsieur Berenger for the summer season. I produce *La Revue en Chemise*. Have you not seen it advertised?"

"I certainly have," I answered, "but as it was a Folies revue, I had no idea you were staging it or that I was auditioning for it." I didn't add that I had long since stopped reading anything about the Folies Bergère, for my previous audition there had given me to understand that there was no chance of my ever appearing in that theater.

"Unbelievable," he said, smiling. "I hope it pleases you to know you will be *Danseuse Étoile* at the Folies Bergère?"

"It is a miracle," I said softly. "I shall love it. I have always dreamed of dancing at the Folies Bergère."

"It pleases me greatly to be able to make your dreams come true." He smiled at me. "I trust you will have a *succès fou*; and now, until tomorrow." He pinched me on the cheek and turned away.

In the cab on the way down the rue Clichy, I asked Mother, "Where do you suppose Monsieur Franck is going to put on his revue?"

"Why at the Étoile Palace, I suppose."

"But he isn't! He's rented the Folies Bergère!" I bounced on the seat like a five-year-old. "Isn't that wonderful? Just think, I'm going to be a star at the Folies Bergère after all."

"Well, well!" Mother took my hand and stroked it gently. "Will wonders never cease! Paris and the Folies Bergère!"

"I hope I'm good enough," I said nervously. "I hope I won't disgrace Monsieur Staats."

"You won't," she answered cheerfully. "Just do your best. Did you have any dinner?"

"No," I admitted. "Nor any lunch either."

"I'll scramble some eggs," she told me as I paid the driver. "We can eat the breakfast brioches and have some hot chocolate. Set the table on the roof, dear," she told me a few minutes later as she stirred the eggs on the electric plate. "We can eat outdoors under the stars and the moon. It's almost as bright as day. This is a night for you to remember, Regina. Don't forget to say a little prayer of thanks. Tomorrow I will write your father that your dream has come true. You are going to star at the Folies Bergère. I declare it's almost too pat. What do we do now that we've come to the happy ending?"

"I've no idea," I admitted. "Keep going, I suppose. Are those eggs ready? I'm starved."

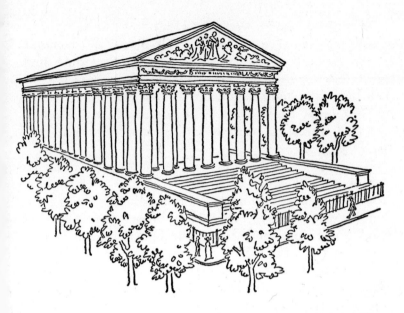

chapter 17:   *Paris Debut*

"Seven-thirty," Mother said briskly, coming into my bed-room the following morning and pulling up the shades. "It's raining cats and dogs," she told me cheerfully. "You'll need galoshes and a raincoat."

I groaned. I sat up and shuddered at the sight of the Niagara of water outside my window. It pelted down on the roof as if shot out of guns. I took a shower, feeling as though I had turned on the heavens, for the water was barely luke-warm and came in heavy spurts rather than in a fine warm spray.

My breakfast *croissant* was hot and crusty, the coffee, rich with cream, but I couldn't eat. I was too excited.

"You'll be hungry in the middle of rehearsal," Mother told me as I shrugged into a raincoat. "Will you need me?" I shook my head.

"I may be late," I warned. "Don't you dare call the police."

"Of course not." She smiled. "No reason to, now I know where you are and what you're doing. I'll cable your father and then write him a long letter. Have a good day."

"Keep your fingers crossed," I begged. "I may get fired. If not, I hope I get home before tomorrow afternoon, but I doubt it."

The morning air was fresh and moist along the Boulevard des Italiens. I loved the quiet loneliness of each person hurrying on, intent on his or her own business. The gray sky and the driving rain seemed to make of each one of us a small human craft in an unknown sea of human emotions.

At the Folies the doorman smiled reassuringly when I said, "Miss Devi," and gave me the keys to my dressing room. It was dank and lonely. There was a star on the door, but only rickety wicker furniture inside. Glaring white frosted bulbs surrounded the mirror, and the whole room could have done with a thorough cleaning. It was lonely and depressing. I changed into a leotard morosely and tied my practice slippers carefully. Then, slipping on my quilted blue silk robe, I picked my way down to the stage, somehow arriving under it, to the surprise of several electricians, who showed me the way up. For this reason I appeared quite suddenly amidst the group on stage which had been watching the staircase down which I was supposed to be coming. After many joking explanations as to why I had come up instead of down, the rehearsal got started.

Everyone else was limbered up and ready to work. It was my first experience with a company rehearsal, and only then did I realize that a nine o'clock rehearsal was not a lesson, but a period of actual dancing, and that I should have been warmed up and ready to perform after at least half an hour of *barre* exercises. I was lucky that the ballet master was busy arranging the grouping of the corps de ballet so I managed to get in some warm-up work. I resolved to be an hour early thereafter and ready to dance my best at the precise moment for which a rehearsal was called.

"Mademoiselle Devi"—M. Franck touched my shoulder— "we will go over your solos in the foyer. Please to come." I followed obediently, and for three hours labored mightily. The ballet master was a wizard. When I found myself with a measure left over or too short a count for a movement I wanted to do, he would let me struggle until he was quite sure what it was I was trying to accomplish, and then, through his superior knowledge of dance, he would fit the desired steps together like a precision watchmaker.

At one o'clock M. Franck told me to stop and get some lunch. I was due at Madame Paquin's at two. "Return here *immédiatement, s'il vous plaît*," he told me. "You know the house of Paquin?" I nodded, but he moved away before I could say Mme. Paquin was dressing me already for the *réclame*. I changed in the dreary dressing room and, quite forgetting to eat, took a cab to Mme. Paquin's. Getting into the establishment took a bit of doing, as there was a new doorman, and I suppose I looked more like an employee than a customer after the morning's workout.

Once inside, I was greeted warmly by one of the *vendeuses*, who knew me quite well. However, she had to turn me over to a hostess, and like a small lost sheep I pattered after the tall, sleekly groomed female, who towered over me and moved as if on roller skates. Finally I found myself in an enormous mirrored room with concealed lighting, soft armchairs covered with green damask, and a gray-green carpet as luxurious as silk velvet. A glass of sherry and biscuits appeared magically. This must, I thought, be one of the fitting rooms reserved for the elite. I was quite impressed. I had never been in one before.

Mme. Paquin drifted in to the room, tall, serene, regal. Her white hair was piled high on her head, and glistened in the lights. She greeted me cordially and congratulated me on having won a solo role at the Folies. When my first costume appeared and was put on me, she gave it her full attention. She had designed a gypsy costume like that of a wood sprite. Its iridescent chiffon gleamed red and green and gold as I moved. Draped, carefully fitted over the bust and shoulders, it clung to my body at the hips, then drifted out in torn wisps to my knees. She bent and ripped it high on the right thigh. She shuddered at the idea of long silk opera stockings, and tossed them aside. My feet were to be bare. My head was garlanded with leaves on an elastic band. One last look . . .

"There is still too much costume!" She came forward, and deftly extricating several pins, yanked out the crepe de Chine lining, leaving only the shimmering folds of the silk between me and the public. She moved back. "Better, much better," she murmured. "Scissors, please." The click-clack of the scissors, the cold steel against my flesh, made me shiver. "Ah, voilà!" She stepped back. I looked at the mirror. I was clad in silken rags which clung to my body and dripped only part way to my knees. It was exactly right. As I moved, trying an *arabesque*, a kick, at her command, I wondered just what it was she had done that made the bunchy, rather ridiculously antiquated Isadora Duncan draped toga tunic into a flowing silken sheath which had a vaguely wanton air about it.

"Make two exactly alike," she bade the deferential modistes who had watched her with expressions half fearful but wholly admiring. "I will be back," she told me. "The Phryne costume is uniquely beautiful. I am sure you will be pleased. This one is to your satisfaction?" I nodded, hardly believing my ears. Could this be I, being asked by Madame Paquin herself if I was content?

When she had gone, I stood, dazed, happily enjoying the misty feeling the sherry had produced, thanks to my empty stomach and my morning's exercise. More silk was brought. I was pinned, pleated, pushed and pulled mercilessly. I said *ouch* automatically and turned on demand. At last the second costume came off, looking the very twin of the first one. The modistes hurried away. My shaking knees beat together like castanets, my legs buckled, my ankles turned. In bra and tight *cache-sexe* I was practically naked. I searched out my clothes from under cascades of shimmering silken material and was about to put them on when the room was invaded by two men in uniform who gathered up the bolts of material rapidly and eyed me coldly as I scolded at their intrusion on my privacy.

"It is of no moment to us to see your nakedness," one of them said to me with a fishy eye. "If you are concerned, cover yourself. In this establishment it seems all women are always naked, and all are the same. Each has one head, two arms, and two legs. What would you?" He thrust several yards of chiffon at me to use as a shawl. "*Allez en*," he snapped, "there is no time to dress. Outside, Mees. A customer who pays American dollars is coming to this room." I was hustled out into a back corridor most unceremoniously, still undressed and protesting under my filmy covering.

"Where do I go then?" I demanded, confronted with a dark, dingy hall, dusty windows, a locked door. No longer was I in the "front"; now I was in the rear, where the employees worked, sewed, and prepared the exquisite creations known as Paquin *originales*.

"It makes no difference where you go or what you do," they explained. "You must await Madame's convenience.

Rest *tranquille,* you sadly need all the looks you have got."
With these words of wisdom, they left me to wait. I stood
around awhile, laid my clothes on a window sill, and cautiously pushed at the barred iron door. It was very warm.
A little air, I thought, would be pleasant. Perhaps the door
opened on a fire escape and I could go out on it. I pushed
harder. It moved with a blood-curdling rasp and tore itself
from my grasp. I gave a little scream. In place of a fire escape
was empty space in the shape of a dark open well, exactly
right for a murder mystery in which the corpse would never
be found. I recoiled exactly as any heroine should, and in my
fright rushed down the dark corridor to where a dim blue
light was burning. It proved to be over another door. I
turned the knob very gingerly, but this time before my daz-
zled gaze was a great workroom with long tables, brilliant
lights, and dozens of chattering girls sewing on mountainous
billows of material of all colors. Silks, satins, and laces
streamed from great bolts. Every table was a hive of activity.
On seeing me, a hush fell. I realized I must explain myself.

"I was being fitted," I told them, "when the room was
needed for someone who would p-pay," I stammered. "I did
not know wh-where to go . . . may I come in here?"

There was a restless murmur, I hoped of approval. I slid
into a seat at a table. "You are a model?" The girl on my
right asked. It was easier to say *yes* than to try to explain I
was a dancer, a sort of non-paying customer, dressed free for
advertising purposes, so I said *yes.* She was sewing red se-
quins deftly on to what seemed endless yards of red chiffon.

"May I help?"

She looked skeptical. "Is it that you can sew? These must
be done a certain way."

"Of course I can sew," I said indignantly. "Give me a
thimble and needle and thread. I'll show you." She passed
them over indulgently and snaked out some material. "The

knot under the sequin, two passes of the needle through the hole, a lock stitch, and cut the thread on the wrong side. *Comprends?*"

"I understand," I said, and proceeded to sew on a sequin, then two, then three.

"*Pas mal*," she said. "Not bad at all, and you are quick. Why do you not join us here? Would it not be a better life? Models have much trouble. It is not a good thing to dress up in such fine clothes. You get ideas. Soon, though, you are old and you have no job and there is nothing you can do but starve or go bad. If you are good with the needle, you can work till you die in your bed."

I nodded. I sewed, I chatted, and I listened. These girls were friendly, smart, and witty. Suddenly loud voices shattered our calm, then a shriek. "*Elle est tombée. Elle est tuée. Quel dommage.* She was so young. What to do?"

At first the clamor seemed to have nothing to do with me. Then, suddenly, as I heard the words, "She is nowhere, I tell you. The door is wide, she has fallen. Here are her clothes," I realized it was I who was supposed to have fallen, that it was my clothes someone had found. I stood up just as Mme. Paquin came hurrying in. "So there you are," she said. "Sewing, too. You have good sense. Come, my dear, we are ready for you."

"Come back whenever you like," the girls told me as I left, and I nodded.

Mme. Paquin made many costumes for me, and every spare moment that I had to wait during my fittings, I spent in the workroom. I learned to fagot exquisite fragments of velvet together with gold thread to make material for evening dresses, to embroider on chiffon, and to cover a hat frame with pearly velvet.

The Phryne costume was almost transparent silk georgette which exactly matched my skin. I looked quite naked. For the rest, it was nothing but dripping crystal fringe some five inches deep, such as is often seen on expensive lamp shades. Later on *The Tatler* published a picture of me in the costume with the caption, "Mlle. Nila Devi of the Folies Bergère, Paris. Undressed by Paquin."

It was nearly five o'clock by the time I got back to the Folies. Everyone was taking a break, and I was thankful for the delicious hot brioches and *café au lait* which I was offered from a small boxlike cart on wheels pushed around by a boy in a white coat.

From this moment on my days were the same as my nights. I danced and danced and danced. Whenever I stopped dancing, I napped on piles of coats at the theater or in bed at home or on the couch in my dressing room. When I wasn't dancing or sleeping, I was trying on costumes or being photographed. Sunday was a day of rest, as rehearsal did not start till 3:00 P.M., so Mother and I went to church at the Madeleine. On returning home, I found a cable of congratulations from my father. I read it over and over. Then I wrote him a long letter and took a nap.

Rehearsals were in costume now. Viglia and Teresita, a South American dance team of considerable fame, had been engaged to do a tango, and there was consternation when it was found that the female half was to have a baby. Forbidden to dance, she moped in a box while her husband tried out various partners. I was not too happy at being chosen to dance with him, but I did my best, though I always felt like a silly pretender as I swooped and glided through an exhibition tango in a long evening dress and wearing high heels.

The days passed, and I neither knew nor cared what went on in the world. One night, sitting out on the roof, my mother said, "Regina, I declare, you are eating breakfast before you go to bed and going to the theater before it is time for you to eat breakfast. I hope when the show opens you'll get onto some kind of proper schedule. Are you eating anything besides *croissants* and coffee at four in the morning?"

"I don't know," I said vaguely. "I don't seem to be hungry at all."

"I can't say I'm surprised," she admitted. "You're living on another plane entirely."

And then my out-of-the-world period was over and the dress rehearsal loomed up. It lasted nearly eight hours, and a great deal had to be cut out of the show. There was applause, recrimination, wrong lighting cues. The curtain came down in the middle of my dance. A hammer fell on stage. I stumbled into the footlights. At last opening night arrived, and I was still alive. My dressing room had American Beauty roses blooming bravely in a great glass vase. They came from my father. The room was clean and bright. My costumes hung on the wall. There was a sheet on the floor. My mother was my dresser. We had brushed aside the idea of a maid. I wanted her and she wanted to be with me.

The overture. The call, "On stage, Miss Devi. *La Feria.*" In the wings the stuffy, musty smell. The sudden glare of footlights. The spotlight, almost blinding in intensity, the strangeness of crowding scenery, the nearness of the corps de ballet. I was hemmed in physically and mentally, but I danced. The audience applauded politely, and I breathed a sigh of relief. Next the tango. Again a good hand. M. Viglia bowed and bowed, always to the stage box. He drew me forward punctiliously and kissed my hand, but he had eyes only for the box. Later I learned that the lovely dark-eyed girl leaning so far forward was his wife, and that he yearned for but one thing, to have her beside him, sharing in his applause.

After the intermission came the ballet of Phryne. This was my dance, the dance I loved. I dressed, trembling and tearful. Mother gently patted the tears off my cheeks. She didn't scold about streaking mascara or say I was silly to weep. I kept saying, "Oh, Mother, I'm afraid I shan't dance well enough. It's such a lovely ballet."

"Why not practice a bit then?" she asked practically. "Over here, by your father's roses. Try an *arabesque*, that long slow one." The moment I began to move, I felt serene and confident. I feasted my eyes on the red roses. I bent to smell their rich garden fragrance. I felt as if my father held my hand. I looked at Mother, and she smiled. She understood.

The call for *Le Bain de Phryné* came. My mother wrapped me in the gleaming folds of my scarlet cape and led me down the stairs. The curtain rose, billowed up and aside. The audience was a dull blur. The stage was amber, the spotlight, blue. The music called. I saw my judges at their desk, high above me. I moved on stage. Then, at their command, my cloak was torn from me. I stood almost naked before the law. The music seemed to force me into moving, into making a dramatic plea for my purity. I danced, I retreated into the character. There were no footlights, tinsel, or applause. I was Phryne before her judges, passionately declaring herself to be a virgin, pure, blameless, and undefiled.

At the end I stood with bowed head, hands clasped on my breast, awaiting the verdict. At a nod from the judges my cape was wrapped carefully about me and I was led to the staircase, freed of stain of shame or crime. I walked up the stairs, chin up, shoulders square, my virginity upheld by court of law. Acquitted, I climbed up, up, out of sight, as the curtain was lowered. I was astounded when I found myself face to face with the dirty stagehands, waiting to help me down the ladder backstage. It was all so sudden, so prosaic, I could have wept. Reality was hard to take. I was clumsy and nervous as I crept down the ladder.

194

M. Franck was waiting in the wings. "*Vite, vite!*" he commanded. "You must take a bow." Only then did I hear the noisy clatter which was surrounded and then surmounted by a strange hissing sound. I backed away from him. I avoided his reaching hands. I burst into tears.

"No," I sobbed. "I won't go out there and be hissed. If I'm that bad, I'll just go home and never, never dance again." I started for the stairs. People made way for me as they saw the tears streaming down my face, my hands gesturing them aside.

"What is this? She is ill? *Malade?* Perhaps she has hurt herself and suffers?" I heard the remarks, but they meant nothing to me.

"You must take a bow." M. Franck had me by the shoulders. He was pushing me before him to the stage. "*Qu' as-tu?*" he demanded. "Why do you weep?"

"I have failed," I sobbed, turning suddenly in his arms and burrowing into his shirt front. "Do you not hear the people going *sss-sss?* They are hissing me."

"They do not hiss." He pushed me from him and shook me. "What idiocy has taken possession of you? They shout, '*Bis.*' They wish you to dance again. Come, little one, smile. All is well. You have had a most extraordinary success." At this instant he caught sight of the lipstick and mascara on his shirt front. "How explain this?" he demanded. "My wife is a person of the greatest jealousy. *Alors,* we will show them, and her as well." The applause continued, even, rhythmical, steady. The word *bis,* now that I knew what it was that the audience was hissing, no longer terrified me. I even heard a few shouted *encores,* which heartened me. M. Franck drew me on stage. Dramatically he pushed me forward. He explained my tears, he gestured to his smeared shirt front. He laughed, he kissed my hand. The audience applauded, half amused, half skeptical, almost certain it was

195

all an act, but willing to go along with the unconventional bit of byplay.

"Well, Regina, your debut is over." Mother, who had been watching from the orchestra, was now fanning herself briskly with a program. "Very nice indeed," she assured me, "and quite an ovation. I told the man next to me by the rail that I was your *maman,* and he kissed my hand and sent you his compliments. I shall write your father. He simply must come over now. He's been promising long enough." I nodded agreement.

There was a furious knocking on the dressing-room door. I opened it to a sea of smiling faces. Congratulations, flowers, telegrams.

"Consider, *Mademoiselle,* a contract at the Moulin Rouge."

"*Attends, Mademoiselle,* M. Mayol, in person, wishes to speak with you."

"Rehearsal for principals at eleven."

"Photographs at two P.M. for *Le Bain de Phryné.*"

"A fitting at five at Paquin."

"A little party now, at the Rat Mort. Your *maman,* of course!"

And so it went. Heady, exciting, furiously paced.

"Truly a *succès fou,*" M. Franck told us, smiling and bowing.

"I never dreamed it would be so much fun," I confided to Mother as she helped me dress for the party.

"Nor did I. This is the life!" she answered.

At the Rat Mort I met Anna Held, at that time an important musical-comedy star, who told me I was quite talented. I met Jack Johnson, a tall and handsome Negro, then the boxing champion of the world, and his white wife. He foxtrotted with me on the tiny square of dance floor, and told me that soon, he, too, would be on the Folies Bergère program. He held me easily in his arms, though I was dangling in midair like a rag doll, my feet some twelve inches above the floor. He seemed to think he was dancing with me, and it didn't seem quite polite to explain that he was merely carrying me around like a stuffed puppet.

Mother was in a huddle with a superbly groomed woman when I returned to the big table laden with orchids. The woman handed me one of the corsages to pin on my shoulder and a glittering glass of champagne. I smiled and nodded my thanks courteously.

"I am giving your *maman* good advice as to how to keep your innocent youth and beauty unspoiled in the midst of this cynical world of the theater," she explained.

"Thank you, Madame," I said politely, and then to Mother, "who is she?"

"Mata Hari," Mother whispered. "She has the dressing room next to yours. She seems like a nice, considerate woman. Eat your chicken all up, dear, before you drink that champagne, or you'll get tipsy."

chapter 18:   *Danseuse Étoile*

Now THAT I was a star at the Folies, I was in demand for
after-theater performances, which added considerably to my
earnings. I still attended ballet class, but it was with the professional dancers at eleven o'clock. I would have preferred
to stay with the students whom I knew, but nine o'clock
class was too early after the frequent late nights.

M. Staats was easier one moment and harsher the next,
now that I was a professional. I worked harder than ever,
but I received less praise. One day when I was scolded, I
burst into tears. "Temperament does not become you," he
told me. "You need to be criticized. All this praise in the
papers will go to your head. If I do not scold you, you will
soon begin to believe you are as good as the critics say you
are, Miss Danseuse Étoile."

"The audience applauds like crazy," I tossed my head.

198

"The audience is a big silly animal," he warned me. "It applauds dogs, horses, monkeys, acrobats, and fat tenors. We are not talking of applause, but of your *arabesque. Allons*, straight knees, nice shoulders, a good back. *And* one . . . *and* two . . ." We were off.

This hard work paid off. At rehearsals the show was pulled apart and put together again. I was given a solo on point in the finale. An adorable white tulle costume with garlands of rosebuds was designed and made on the spot by some of the *midinettes* I knew at Paquin's. The ballet master complimented me on my *bourrées* and on my straight knees. He said I had a nice point and I carried myself well. "The arms," he informed me, "were truly classic." I had been well trained.

My stock went up as evidence of my ability as a ballet dancer became apparent. A new partner who could tango better than I was found for M. Viglia, and a ballet was built around my toe solo. I was happier than I had ever been in my whole life, for I adored dancing on point in a ruffly white tutu.

Mail from home was the delight of our lives, but it also held disappointments. My father, who had promised faithfully to come over after my debut, wrote that he couldn't. Aunt Barb wasn't well enough to leave, and several business deals were pending. "Perhaps in six months." Mother cried a little and I was sobered. Six months. Why, in six months I would be at the Alhambra in Algiers, dancing *Lysistrata*. In addition, I had signed contracts with the Moulin Rouge to appear in another revue and the Concert Mayol to dance *L'Idole Turquoise*. The agent Martinelli had taken me under his wing and was even now dickering with the Jardin d'Hiver in Budapest. I had become a property to be sold to the highest bidder. All I did now was dance, model gowns in restaurants or at the races, be photographed or painted. The fun of dancing was rapidly being reduced to a dollars and cents estimate. When? Where? How long? How much?

The next letter I opened was postmarked London. It was from my French teacher at Dana Hall, Mlle. Reuche, who was conducting a tour. Oh, this was more like it! I crowed in delight. "Mother, listen! Mademoiselle Reuche will be in Paris the twelfth. Why that's tonight! She wants tickets to the show, and then she will bring the girls backstage. Oh, glory, won't it be fun?"

I called the theater and arranged for third-row seats in the orchestra and left backstage passes for them at the box office. I called Mademoiselle, and we gabbled French as naturally as we once spoke English. All was arranged. That evening was, for me, the peak of my success. Over the brilliance of the footlights I could see seven or eight high-pompadoured young ladies, wearing white shirtwaists, with high-boned collars. The little, short, stout gray-pompadoured lady beside them wore black taffeta. I danced as I had never danced before. I milked my applause with fluttering eye lashes and an extra *bourrée*. I smiled and smiled at my classmates, and even ripped open a bouquet and threw a barrage of roses directly into their laps.

Backstage I was all atwitter. "*Restes tranquille*," M. Franck implored me, "or you will forget." I steadied myself, remembering the dreadful night that I had seen the woman in the box with a pistol pointed at me. I had frozen in an *attitude*. I didn't know where I was or what I should be doing next. "Move. Improvise. Pirouette! Anything, but move!" The whispered words of the ballet master in the wings fell on deaf ears, but fortunately for me, training took over and the deep freeze I was in gave way to movement of a sort, though I never knew how I finished the dance.

"What happened?" I asked Mother later, my knees buckling under me as I sat down at my make-up table. "And what on earth is this?" I picked up a legal-looking document ornamented with official seals.

"Finish your act," she said wearily. "It's all right now. The gendarmes have taken her away."

Dancing was hardly fun the rest of the evening, but the explanation was even less so. It seems I had been served with a warrant for alienating the affections of the conductor of the orchestra.

"But I have never even spoken to him off stage," I protested.

"You will have to explain that to a judge or probably to a *maître* appointed by the judge." Mother shrugged her shoulders. "We must be in court. It will be a private hearing, I believe, next Friday, at ten A.M. Monsieur Franck will provide us with a lawyer."

I was truly terrified. "What can I say?" I demanded on meeting the lawyer. "It is simply absurd."

"Control yourself, speak softly, and tell the truth," he counseled. "Do not say, 'It is absurd.' That is for the *maître* to decide, not you."

Our visit to court proved incredibly simple. The *maître* who had been appointed to hear our case wore a black robe. He had a pointed black Vandyke beard and sat behind a massive desk in a small private room in the Palais de Justice. The conductor was there, and the woman, shorn of pistol, was there, a matron on one side, a doctor on the other.

The conductor testified that he did not know me personally, that we had never been alone anywhere together, that our only contact was over the footlights when he conducted my music.

My story was the same as his.

Mother corroborated everything, adding explosively that

I never went anywhere socially without her. The *maître* nodded, slightly bored.

The woman then spoke rapidly. I couldn't follow her French too well, but it seemed that I had bewitched her husband. He followed every move I made with careful attention, he never took his eyes from me. In fact, I had taken her husband from her and was a bad woman. Therefore, she had decided I should die, and why not?

Finally the *maître* raised his hand. The doctor, spoke, and I gathered she was *malade* and belonged in *hôpital*. The *maître* asked the conductor a question. Papers were brought in and signed. The woman went away. The *maître* motioned Mother and me forward. It was all over. It was evident I had done no wrong. I would please to excuse the overjealous wife whose mind was not all it should be. He shook hands. The lawyer shook hands. There was no charge. For such a charming lady, it was a pleasure to be of service. He would be present this very evening to applaud me in *Le Bain de Phryné*. The conductor shook hands with me and went to speak with his wife. Mother and I took a cab. She looked tired and shaken.

"Really, Regina," she said. "This is all very peculiar. I had no idea when you became a professional that we would be so tied up that our time was no longer our own, nor our lives, nor even our behavior. I'm not sure I like it."

"I don't either," I admitted. "But it's all part of the theater. We'll have to put up with it, I guess, as long as I'm a professional dancer."

Neither the Paris nor the London papers bothered with my day in court because of an insane gunwoman's charge, but the New York and Boston papers played it up in headlines. Father cabled me to come home at once where I could dance without being shot at. We sent back a cable that I had contracts. That all was well. Not to worry.

Sunday morning Mother and I went to church. I played the matinee, and then we met Mlle. Reuche and her girls for dinner at the Café de la Paix. They seemed just the same, only much, much younger than I remembered. They were friendly, and just a shade patronizing. I had made a wonderful success, but did I really want to dance in places like the Folies and the Moulin Rouge? After all, Diaghileff had a ballet company. Why didn't I join it?

"For the same reason that most American singers go into musical comedy instead of the opera, or painters get hung in small galleries on Fifty-seventh Street instead of at the Metropolitan Art Gallery. I haven't either the training or the ability those Russian dancers have. Diaghileff would laugh his head off if I even applied for the corps. I love to dance, but I am no more comparable to Karsavina than Janey's paintings are to Rembrandt's."

It was hardly tactful, but at that moment I was recognized by a party of very jovial South Americans who seemed to have all the money in the world and were determined to spend it on famous names in the theater. Almost at once a whole basketful of fragrant violets was delivered to our table with their compliments. Much smiling and waving, and eventually hand kissing followed, in which the girls were included. This episode caused me to rise considerably in their estimation, for which I was duly thankful.

We talked music and art, and by the time we said good-by, they had notes on what they *must* see in the Louvre, the Luxembourg, the Musée Guimet, until they protested that they were only tourists and simply couldn't live in art galleries as we seemed to.

My final gesture was to give them all bunches of violets and my personal card to a showing at Madame Paquin's, hoping that the superb salesladies would look down their noses at these tripper Americans, as they had once looked down on me.

"We're out of touch," Mother said later that evening. "Regina, I had no idea how you'd changed. I'm surprised and a little sorry. I'm not at all sure we did right in accepting all these contracts if you really feel that your dancing is mediocre. You sounded so adult, bitter, and cynical that I'm worried."

"You don't need to be," I answered. "When I started out, I was just a nobody from nowhere. In two years, I've made good in a darned difficult profession, but it gets my goat when someone asks why I'm not up there with the greats in the world of ballet. I'm not really a prima ballerina or a *danseuse étoile*. They are just press-agent titles, and I couldn't be so dumb as not to know it, either. The girls were just needling me, and it made me mad. I'm happy just where I am in the theater, for it's where I belong."

"Good," Mother said. "Then you're glad you're going on to the Moulin Rouge, Concert Mayol, and the Alhambra?"

"I'm thrilled," I admitted, "for in Algiers I'll be creating a role. Mother, do you realize what a step up it is to be creating the dances for *Lysistrata's* first performance?" I sighed, then looked up at her. "Oh, Mother, what a fool I am. Why didn't I say something superior like, 'Well, I am getting out of this musical revue rat-race, you know. My manager has just completed an arrangement whereby I will create my own dances in *Lysistrata* in December in Algiers. It is the Maurice Donnay version of Aristophanes' comedy. A first of great importance artistically. I am very proud to have been entrusted with creating the solo role in that particular production.'"

"Why, indeed!" Mother agreed. "Isn't it maddening the way one always thinks of a telling retort or the *mot juste*, just too late?"

chapter 19:   *Starring in Paris, Algiers, and Budapest*

THE BIGGEST SURPRISE when I made my move from the Folies to the Moulin Rouge and began working out my dances with the corps de ballet there was to find myself taken seriously as a choreographer. All my life I had "made up" dances, "regulated" them, or "put them together," but suddenly this type of work was called "choreography" and the ballet master as well as the corps deferred to me. It was a heady and exciting business. I loved it. It made my dancing more personal, more my own. The first time I saw, "Choreography by Nila Devi" in print, my elation knew no bounds. I promptly cut the piece out and mailed it to Mlle. Reuche and her group in Munich. "That'll show 'em," I told Mother, who only raised her eyebrows skeptically.

The Moulin Rouge proved a happy experience, as did the Concert Mayol. Once, standing in the wings, admiring M.

Mayol as he sang (for I was deeply enamored of him), he stopped as he came off to ask anxiously if I could understand the words. I shook my head. "*Non*, the argot is beyond comprehension," I admitted.

"If you had understood, I could not have permitted you to remain," he told me. "After all, you do not yet have eighteen years."

It was while I was at the Concert Mayol that I was plagued by seeing my posters still outside the Folies Bergère and the Moulin Rouge, where substitute dancers were appearing under my name. I attended one performance and called a lawyer. "If they were good dancers," I sputtered, "I wouldn't mind so much, but they're awful. Make the management take my name down outside and off the programs."

He argued that I should be happy over the publicity, but I pointed out that anyone who saw either of them dance and thought it was I would never, never go to see me again. "They're ghastly," I told him, "and the audience knows it. There is no applause."

It took several weeks, but eventually my name disappeared from the theaters in which I was not appearing. Several paintings of me were shown in the Salon, and I was asked to pose for a sculptor. Christmas was a busy time. Many of our London friends came to Paris for vacations, bent on giving us a wonderful time. Father was again in Bermuda, recovering from a serious attack of asthma. He wrote we ought to be thinking of coming home, pointing out that I had gone abroad to *learn* to dance, but that my remaining on as a *professional* had never even been considered. Anyway, money was no longer an object. He had plenty of it for all our needs.

"Your father has something there," Mother agreed. "You'd better have Martinelli figure out a New York engagement. I'll be sorry not to go to Germany or Italy, as he has proposed, but your father is right. We'd better go home after Algiers and Budapest." I felt a little scared. European audiences liked me, but I had no idea if the audiences in the United States would. However, I was much too busy to worry. I was working out my *Lysistrata* solo dances, knowing there would only be three days for rehearsal once I arrived in Algiers.

Packing up, saying good-by to Paris, the theaters in which I had worked, and our pleasant quarters in the rue de Helder made me question the joys of professionalism. When we arrived at the dock and were told that the boat from Marseille to Algiers was not taking passengers this trip because it was too rough, I had a proper tantrum. I shouted I *had* to go, regardless of the "wicked sea." Of course, I would sign a release—anything—if they would let me on board. This the Captain finally agreed to, and Mother and I settled ourselves on a little bench in the center of the deck. The boat cast off its lines, it heaved and wallowed. Mother and I chatted. I looked off at the shore line and turned to speak to her. She was no longer there! Instead, in slow motion, she was rolling down the deck toward the rail. I shrieked "Mother!" then I, too, was gently wafted off my seat to join her on deck. Imprecations flew down from the Captain above us at the wheel, and a covey of sailors grabbed us unceremoniously, and setting us on our feet, escorted us to our stateroom. There we were told we must go to bed.

"In the middle of the day?" Mother protested. But to bed we went, and were tied in with clothesline looped over us. By suppertime we were starved. Feeling like Houdinis, we finally got ourselves untied and out and dressed. Again on deck we fought our way forward, holding onto the ropes. There was no one in the salon, nor was there a vestige of a meal, but we could smell food, and we followed our noses. In the mess hall we were received with consternation and hurried along to the Captain's small private dining room. There he informed us that no provision had been made for passengers as none were to be carried, and anyway, why weren't we in our bunks? It was thought we should be seasick.

"Well, we're not, and we're starved." I eyed the Captain's dinner hungrily. He gave in, and we ate well that night and the following morning.

At the Alhambra I was treated like royalty. My word was law in regard to the ballet scenes. My dressing room was big, airy, clean, and had an adjoining bath. Once again my age did not permit me to attend the performance, for it was *"pas pour les jeunes filles,"* but M. Gemier, the manager, escorted me by the private door between the auditorium and back stage, and I saw the show in a theater where I could perform but where I could not buy a ticket.

Lysistrata was a success, and I began preparing for *Les Saltimbanques*. We had ten days off, and decided on a trip into the desert. I wanted to see the *Ouled Naïls* dance, and Mother wanted to see camels and sand dunes. Before our three-day trip to Bou Saada was over, we had seen everything from burnoosed Arabs, hundreds of miles of yellow dunes, dirty donkeys, horrible leering camels, and scavenger dogs. There were smelly sheep in such herds and droves that Mother swore that once she returned to civilization, never again would a morsel of lamb pass her lips. "Goat!" she ejaculated over her dinner of stew, and demanded anything that didn't smell, even if only dried biscuits.

Outside Bou Saada we were told that a Marabout, a descendant of Mahomet, had a harem of dancing girls, though as a sacred person he had no wives. It seemed he would be pleased to permit me to see his dancers if I, in turn, would dance for him and for them. This was very good news, for in Algiers we had been told that it was difficult for foreigners to see real Oriental dancing. Moreover, they explained, too many white women had gone to visit harems and failed to return. While both the American Consul and the French Consul were quite willing I should *go*, they would take no responsibility for bringing me *back*. "For serious lady anthropologists, yes, but for dancers, no!"

I tackled the British Consul. "I am an artist," I explained. "I am in search of ethnic dance. I am doing *research*. I am a serious student of folk customs!"

Immediately I had his promise that the whole British Army would march to recover me if I failed to reappear in ten days. It gave me a nice feeling of security. Mother shrugged. "It sounds good, even if they don't mean a word of it."

We went by car, and only after I was inside the forbidding turreted white building and standing before Bord-el-Arreredrij, a handsome bearded old man in flowing robes, did I wonder whether it was wise to have come. He had arranged for me to dance before some hundred or more men. Behind a flower-decorated grill I could see hooded figures and hear chatterings and giggles.

I changed behind a screen of hanging Persian rugs. I leaped, I turned, I bent, I pirouetted. My audience watched stolidly. They muttered and consulted one another. I finished in a deep reverence. Immediately I was presented sweets, flowers, scarves, and silver arm bracelets. My clothes were rolled into a bundle and I was escorted to the women's quarters.

There I danced to an audience of women convulsed with mirth. If there had been any aisles, they would have been rolling in them. Everything I did struck them as very funny. They screeched and hugged each other. Finally I was pulled down among them, and one by one they danced for me. They smiled and wiggled and shook their hips and bumped their bellies. Their feet shuffled and never left the floor. I applauded, and all was well.

More scarves, heavy thick sweet coffee, perfumed cigarettes, sticky sweet cakes. No wonder they were soft, languorous, and fat. When I attempted to change back into street clothes, I found there was no privacy. Privacy was nonsense. Weren't we all women? I was dressed by unaccustomed eager hands, hands which found that my whiteness turned pink on being pinched. Only by yowling and pinching back like a tiger cat did I bring this delightful amusement to an end. I never did get my silk stockings back. The last I saw of them they were being worn as long silk mittens.

My presents were put in two lovely baskets, I was patted, kissed, and prayed over. The miles of corridor I trod were scary. I kept wondering if I were on the way out . . . or on the way in. Eventually the iron gates clanged open. There was the car. Mother and chauffeur were sound asleep. They woke, consumed numberless sweet cakes and fruits, and listened to my story.

"Let's go," Mother said suddenly. "I declare, I do believe the desert as well as the dances you describe are very much overrated."

The return voyage to Marseille with the same captain and a boatload of passengers would have been anticlimactic, except that we dined with him in his private room and recounted our adventures, which we exaggerated to impress him.

Before we did anything but pick up our mail, we scrambled aboard the luxurious Orient Express bound for Budapest. I woke early as we were going through the Swiss Alps. I poked Mother, and we saw the sun rise in the most glorious setting of icy rainbow-hued peaks imaginable.

Budapest was a wealthy, artistic city in 1913. Construction of the Jardin d'Hiver had just been finished. I had a good dressing room, but it was still unpainted, and there was no water. A huge bill had been assembled from all over Europe, but because the theater did not yet have a permit from the fire department, only one set of scenery could be hung that night. No changes were allowed.

We learned this the hard way. No one in authority spoke English, French, or German. We spoke no Hungarian. I pulled the manager's evening coattails, but my scenery and curtains did not go up. When my music started, I gave in and rushed on stage. I was doing a *Bacchanale*. During the dance, several blobs of wet plaster fell on me. Once I turned and saw that, instead of my lovely blue semicircle of velvet drapes, I was dancing before a flat of red-coated hunters on horseback and spotted hunting dogs. This so disoriented me that I faltered in my dance. But no one noticed, for suddenly I was surrounded, not by painted black-and-white spotted Dalmatians on a canvas backdrop, but the real thing. The big dogs milled about the stage in confusion. They smelled me, sniffed me, licked me. I screamed, more plaster fell, and one large sandbag broke on the apron of the stage in front of me. Staring over the footlights at a house rocking in delight at the contretemps, I knew failure. At last a merciful curtain fell.

Eventually I was rescued from the mob of performing dogs by their trainer, who, seeing his backdrop, had let them go on stage, assuming that this was his cue. I was apologized to, patted, and my hand kissed. An interpreter promised my own curtains, flowers, extra money, anything, to stop my tears. The next night all went well. My curtains were up, I danced a *Bacchanale* minus dogs and horses. I received an ovation, only one squirt of plaster fell, and the management gave me a party.

I met diplomats: Russian, Hungarian, Turkish. I was

feted. I was curtsied to by everyone who waited on me. We received fabulous presents—jewelry, silver, china. A carriage and pair were at our disposal. I had many suitors, but a Baron Rudas was my favorite. Once he even ordered chunks of dirty brown ice cut out of the Danube so that Mother and I could sail three hundred yards on the famous river.

"Never!" Mother swore. "Never again in this darned country will I say, 'I wish.' It is too confusing when you get what you want, especially if you don't really want it."

When we left the country, our baggage was searched, and all the lovely documents with ribbons and seals we had been given by our friendly "diplomats" who had wined and dined us so zealously were confiscated. Not until the murder a few months later of the heir to the Austrian throne, the Archduke Francis Ferdinand, did we realize that the chances were good that we had been carrying treasonable documents. There had been vigorous arguments at the border, but our American passports were in good order, and eventually we had been allowed to proceed.

"I expect it was confusing," Mother told me, once we were settled in our compartment. "That fat one with the mustaches hanging down to his chin kept saying, 'Americans they are not. The old lady speaks perfect German. Their English is like that of the Britishers. The young one resembles a Russian, while she speaks French with an Italian accent. She is also a ballerina! Who ever heard of an American ballet dancer?' I am very glad we're headed home," Mother added. "I guess it's about time. I expect your father would say that our honeymoon with the dance is over."

"I'm quite willing to go home," I agreed. "It certainly was luck that Lee Shubert saw me dance. Honestly, I never expected an interview like that one. When I was told to go up to his room in the hotel I was terrified, but when I got there, I saw he had no bad intentions. He just had a sore toe, all tied up with a poultice of rags, and was hopping around like an angry canary."

"What did he say?" Mother asked, getting out our tickets and our passports, just in case, as the train was slowing down.

"That I danced very well, and to come see him as soon as I got to New York and that he'd fix me up with a job. Took about a minute and a half. I'm almost sure I caught the elevator that I came up in on its way down."

"Daddy will be pleased," Mother said, smiling. "We'll cable the instant we reach Paris and catch the first boat. Regina, this is ridiculous, but I'm so glad we're going home, I could weep." She dabbed at her eyes. I knew just how she felt. Suddenly I was terribly homesick too. We couldn't get back to the United States fast enough now that we'd made our decision.

chapter 20:   *Home Is the Dancer*

THE TRIP back to the United States was the exact opposite
of the trip abroad. Instead of courting publicity, I shied
away from it. I slept almost all the time, whether I was in
my stateroom or in a deck chair. I appeared just once in public, at the ship's concert. Only for charity would I bestir
myself or be sociable.

Mother and I were so excited to see the Statue of Liberty
that I nearly fell overboard, but not because I was sitting on
the rail posing for pictures. Of course the usual reporters'
demand for "cheesecake" was made when they arrived on
board, and I complied politely on their solemn promise that
as soon as we docked I would be left alone to visit with my
father.

At first we couldn't find him, for he was waiting under the
J's and we had a time convincing him that I was now a *D*,

thanks to all my theatrical baggage coming in under the name Nila Devi. My personal luggage was expedited, though I was told I would have to wait a week or two for Customs' appraisal of my costumes, scenery, jewelry, and gifts.

There was just time for a swift glimpse of New York's skyscrapers and Central Park by taxicab before we settled down to talk in a Pullman drawing room bound for Boston. Father was amused, delighted, and proud of his daughter. I was thrilled to find him in such good health. He didn't cough at all. He seldom even cleared his throat. I had not remembered him as being so distinguished-looking nor so autocratic, but my experiences abroad now made me fully aware of his qualities as a gentleman and a man of substance and integrity. We talked and asked questions. We listened and interrupted each other.

At Back Bay Station, I was given a triumphal welcome by a dozen or more friends. Then we drove back home in separate motor cars. Aunt Barb and Frank, the new man-of-all work, had prepared a festive buffet table on the big veranda. Friends came and went. I danced on the level greensward not once but many times. My friends sat in front of me on the grassy bank. Older folk watched from the broad veranda. My backdrop was the fruit orchard. When evening came, Chinese lanterns were lit, cars were pointed at me from the driveway, their headlights turned on. Dreadful, grating gramophone records sounded thinly in the summer twilight. I danced and danced, wearing my filmy Phryne frock, which traveled everywhere with me in my personal suitcase as a talisman of good fortune.

Late that night we were still talking. Mother was fresh as a daisy. She held one of my father's hands and I, the other as we sat under the stars and relaxed happily, the lights of half a hundred cities twinkling below us, vying with the glittering galaxies above.

The two weeks I spent at home were pure delight. I rode Starlight, going down to the riding school to which he had eventually been sold. I talked dance, art, music, and museums with friends. I reveled in the big house, the delicious New England food: crisp fishballs, baked beans, and brown bread filled with plump raisins; fish chowder and Indian pudding. But first, last, and always was the fact that Father, Mother, and I were together again. I had gone abroad. I had learned to dance. I had made a successful professional debut. Now I was a young woman, capable of earning my own living, and soon I would proceed to do so.

Almost regretfully I packed my bags, said good-by to Mother and Father, and went back to New York. I called on Mr. Lee Shubert.

Because he was out of town and I preferred to make no other contacts until I had seen him personally, I did considerable sight-seeing. I walked about, visited the art museums, saw the monuments, and craned my neck at the high buildings.

Eventually I received an appointment with Mr. Shubert. He took me backstage at the Winter Garden. He gave me tickets to the show, and I marveled at his new star, Marilyn Miller, who was appearing in the leading role of *Sunny*. The Winter Garden had a hit in her; Mr. Shubert didn't need me. He promised to call me in a day or two. Nowadays that would mean never. In twenty-four hours Mr. Shubert did call me. He had arranged for me to meet Mr. William Morris who wanted a star for Ida Fuller's Ballet, which he was staging at the Jardin de Danse, atop the New York Theater in Times Square.

Once I began rehearsing, I was completely happy. I had three numbers which I was free to choreograph as I pleased. Miss Fuller handled the ballet and lights and instructed me in the *Fire Dance*. I never used sticks as Loie

216

Fuller did, preferring merely to wave my scarves. Miss Fuller offered no suggestions as to the dance itself, taking over merely at the end, when I was to flare up, burn, and crumble to ashes.

It was the first time I had ever worked on a grating over brilliant hot lights and a blower. The first time I looked down and saw a man's leering face under my feet, I screamed in terror. It took some explaining for me to understand that the poor man crouched sweating under the wire grating was no intruder but a necessary part of my dance. He it was who blew my scarves high and focused the changing lights on them as I writhed and bent this way and that in tormented grace. Gradually he would cut down the force of the blowers until I lay in an unearthly grayish-lavender light, seemingly only a tiny heap of dead ashes.

I also danced a Greek dance in soft silken tunic with the ballet, and did a *pas de deux* in blocked slippers with lovely Thelma Carleton as my partner. Because there was no Madame Paquin in New York, I proceeded to make my own costumes. I knew how, and they cost so little that I could have as many as I wanted.

My unbridled enthusiasm for dancing and my desire to give my all rather annoyed my partner. "Do you have to work so hard and so fast?" she demanded. "At this rate you'll burn yourself out in a couple of years."

How to end the *pas de deux* was a question. I wanted to be lifted high. She was strong and graceful, but complained, "You're like a greased frog. You're always a little ahead of me in the lifts."

"Then run with me," I suggested, and we ended up our dance circling the block-long ballroom floor with fast toe *bourrées* and long flying jumps, and because I flew up and down with the greatest of ease, our exit roused even the apathetic, half-drunk diners to wild applause.

At that time the Jardin de Danse was Diamond Jim Brady's hangout, but he gave out more dollar bills with packages of cigarettes than he did diamonds, though he himself was decked out like a lighted theater marquee. Wherever he was, there was always a group of avid gold-diggers around him, fawning and courting his favor.

The run was successful. Father came down to see me dance. Mother was just recovering from a minor operation and couldn't travel. Father was considerably amused to find that no one believed him to be my own father. "Father, indeed!" one of my ballet girls jibed. "A swell old gent with a fur coat and a Vandyke beard beauing you round and buying you presents is your *father!* Who do you think you're kidding? He's your Sugar Daddy. Your own personal Diamond Jim Brady."

It was the greatest satisfaction to me to see Standing Room Only signs up every night. Mr. Shubert came by with Mr. Morris one evening and congratulated me. At the end of the run I was summoned by Mr. Martin Beck. He had a brilliant and lovely singer, Madame Eva Gauthier, whom he wished to send out on his Keith-Orpheum Circuit. She had seen me dance and thought we might be able to work out an act together.

It proved a most auspicious partnership. In about two months we were ready with a vaudeville turn we called "Songmotion." Eva Gauthier would sing, I would dance to her voice. Because she had lived in Java and was enamoured of Javanese music and I had had some experience with Indian dancing in Paris, we worked out a heady combination of Javanese and Malayan songs and dancing. The costumes and music were to be authentic. Mr. Beck looked over the act and gave it his approval. We signed our contracts. Scenery was designed and made up. A stage man-

218

ager, Mr. Smith, and a conductor were procured, and away we went.

Our first performance in Davenport, Iowa, was a disaster. We were booed, laughed at, and made targets for pennies and programs. Almost hysterical, Eva and I changed into street clothes and sat down with Mr. Smith and the conductor to discuss what to do. We had a fifty-two week tour ahead, but if this was a preview of audience reaction, the Gauthier-Devi act wouldn't last two minutes in a big city.

The stage manager, Mr. Smith, was outspoken. He took Madame Gauthier apart first. "Take off that horse's head thing you're wearing and get rid of that sarong with its tail between your legs. Scrap that whiny music. You're a good-looking woman. Put on your best evening gown, sing the Bell song from *Lakmé*, and you'll get a good hand." Madame promptly fainted.

On being revived, she stalked out of the room, announcing, "We'll close before I prostitute my art."

I came next. According to Mr. Smith I looked bowlegged as I moved my feet and legs in Javanese fashion. Even he had had to laugh. My native costumes were ugly. Why did I have four eyebrows? And if I *could* really dance, why did I just wiggle and jiggle about? Why didn't I kick and do back bends and pirouettes?

Not being as sold on ethnic dance as Eva was, I assured him that there was nothing I liked better than doing high *arabesques*, *battements*, and pirouettes. I suggested we add to our act some of my own specialties from Europe. An Indian dance, a plastique dance, a czardas, and a toe solo. I would whip up the costumes in nothing flat from bargain-basement material. I would coax Eva to sing opera and forego the lovely gold-leather headdress which Mr. Smith

219

insisted made her look like a horse. No use telling him it was meant to, for it was a horse god headdress. Mr. Smith was already too annoyed to see anything funny about anything.

Madame talked about art. She talked about culture. She insisted our job was to "raise standards." I didn't agree. Our job was to entertain, and if what we did was above the heads of the audience, then why not lower it a bit? Were opera music and ballet such a bad combination? Why not give the audience what it wanted, not what *we* thought it ought to have. She was hard to convince, for she was an innovator and a cultured artist. While I yearned only to please and to perform, she wanted to originate and instruct. I was determined to be admired and applauded, where she was content to be respected and rejected.

It took a week to reorganize ourselves over Madame's pained protests, but even she was pleased when, at our first performance, she was bravo'd and had to give an encore. She even forgave my dancing a toe solo in a pale blue tutu with crimson poppies on it to her "Indian Love Call" because the audience liked it so much. *Variety* announced our acceptance in no uncertain terms a few weeks later, saying, "Gauthier and Devi repeated their previous success." Once we had added a Sicilian love song, a Greek fantasy, and a French *valse* to our Malayan and Javanese songs and dances, we had six or seven curtain calls, and often persistent applause from a delighted audience delayed the show several minutes.

Week by week we gained assurance and poise. Good press notices and good reviews gave us confidence. Eva began to lecture on Javanese music before women's clubs, and I was called upon to demonstrate steps and movements of the dances. Before long we were successful vaudevillians in the afternoon and evening and serious lecturers at morning

musicals and luncheons. Even I began lecturing on choreography and showing how a dance was born.

We met many interesting people in the cities we visited
and managed a good bit of sight-seeing as we crossed the
country, our private car hitched on to any old freight train
that was handy. There was no rest. If we weren't traveling
Sundays, we played matinees and evening performances as
usual. More than once only half dressed, Madame clutching
her corsets under her arm and I still in tights under my winter coat, we panted up the station platform at midnight to
catch a train being held for us.

We traveled up and down and across the United States
and Canada. We appeared in New Orleans, in Winnipeg, in
Seattle, in Los Angeles, and in every city in between it
seemed. Hurry, hurry, rehearse, perform, practice! It was
the most thrilling of all, though, when we were rushed to re-
place Roshanara at the Salt Lake City Orpheum. This loveliest of English girls, well trained in authentic Indian dancing, was being booed just as we had been a few weeks earlier
in Davenport. Somehow it made us feel we were real troup-
ers now that we had managed to succeed despite such an
inauspicious beginning. Eva and I congratulated ourselves
that we had got off so easily. All the audience had thrown
at us was pennies. In Salt Lake they had thrown rotten tomatoes and oranges at the lovely Roshanara.

When the fifty-two weeks were up, neither Madame nor I
wanted another tour. We thanked God and our stage manager that we had succeeded, but neither of us wanted to remain in vaudeville. Madame Gauthier decided to combine
teaching with concerts. She suggested I go into concert too,
modeling myself on the lovely Angna Enters. I was undecided. Musical comedy seemed more my field. I decided to
do nothing until I had had a real old-fashioned Christmas at
home, and back I went to family, Christmas tree, and the

fun and thrill of racing along in a pung, my father beside me, as we sped over the hard-packed snow, ice spraying in our faces from the horse's hoofs.

Always before this my contracts had forbidden sports of any kind for fear I might injure myself. Now I tobogganed and skated to my heart's content. But how right those contracts were! In less than a month I had done my first and only double somersault in the Boston Arena, catching the tip of my skate in a hole in the defective ice as I skimmed onto the rink in an *arabesque,* and I was no longer a toe dancer, but a young woman in a specially constructed shoe.

"At least a year before you can go on your toes again," the doctor said, and signed my claim, since I was well insured against injury.

World War I was being fought in Europe. There were ambulance units going to France. I spoke French. I, too, would go. I saw myself a heroine, an angel of mercy, back in my beloved France. No longer would I be a performer, rather would I be a Florence Nightingale, driving an ambulance and ministering to the wounded. I learned to drive an automobile. I studied motor mechanics. I took a course in Red Cross First Aid. My instructor was a tall blond man, who wore a Phi Beta Kappa key. He was a Southerner, quiet, gentle, conservative. He was also Assistant Dean at Harvard Medical School. I received 98 in all three of my courses. The tall blond man asked if he might call when the course was completed. I said *yes.*

Chestnut Hill raised money for an ambulance, but I never went abroad to drive it. Instead I fell in love and married the tall blond Phi Beta Kappa. When he went to Washington, I went too. He was a first lieutenant attached to the Surgeon General's Office and served as liaison officer between it and the General Staff. I kept busy housekeeping and writing. In the evenings I typed for him at the War Office build-

222

ings. A year later our son was born, an event which effectually closed my career as a performing artist and started me on one as a doctor's wife, mother, and writer.

Dancing and writing about dancing has been the joy of my life. I have taken pride in good craftsmanship and enjoyed every moment of the hard work which led to my modest success. I had a dream of being a star and I saw it realized. I was one of the lucky ones who had the will—and who found the way—thanks to loving, understanding parents.